THE **HEART** AND **SOUL** OF **CULTURE**

How to Save Your Bottom Line by Making the Transformation to a Conscious Business

THE **HEART** AND **SOUL** OF **CULTURE**

How to Save Your Bottom Line by Making the Transformation to a Conscious Business

Tom Hinton and Barbara Yager

Blue Carriage
Publishing Company

Published by: Blue Carriage Publishing Company
Post Office Box 503016, San Diego, California 92150-3016

HINTON, TOM, Author
YAGER, BARBARA, Co-Author
The Heart and Soul of Culture: How to Save Your Bottom Line by Making the Transformation to a Conscious Business
Hinton, Tom, and Yager, Barbara

ISBN: 5-5 978-0-9835032-7-9

BUSINESS & ECONOMICS / Organizational Development
BUSINESS & ECONOMICS / Workplace Culture

Schools, companies, professional groups, clubs, and other organizations may qualify for special terms when ordering quantities of this title. For information, email Info@CRIGlobalCAPS.com.

Editing and Book Design by *Nita Helping Hand?* www.NitaHelpingHand.com
Cover by KAM Designs, www.KAM.design

Table of Contents

Foreword

By Dr. Tony Alessandra, Ph.D.

When I was a doctoral student at Georgia State University, two things my professors emphasized were the importance of knowing the facts and, secondly, understanding the Culture of an organization. While the world has changed dramatically over the past 40 years since I began my own business, two things have remained constant. First, how leaders gather data and information, and how to use that data and information to improve a company's performance which is essential to its long-term success. Second, Culture matters because it defines who you are as an organization and, equally important, how your customers define you!

As the Founder of www.Assessments24x7.com – a company that offers online assessments, including the widely used DISC profile, the Hartman HVP, Motivators (Values/PIAV) assessment, as well as several specialty, developmental and hiring/selection assessments – I know firsthand that people change; and, therefore, organizations change.

But for leaders to understand what changed and how those changes will impact its customer relationships, brand recognition, employee performance, competition and financial results is paramount to ensuring its long-term relevance and success in the marketplace.

Several years ago, when authors and speakers Tom Hinton and Barbara Yager first told me about The *Heart and Soul of*

Culture book project and their Culture Assessments, I was excited and intrigued. I knew their book could help every company and organization better understand their Culture and improve their performance through their people. I also knew the first step in that process was a tried-and-proven assessment that could reveal an organization's strengths and opportunities for improvement from a Culture perspective. The *Heart and Soul of Culture* offers you a roadmap to understanding your Culture and using it to strengthen and transform your business results.

Every leader has seen his or her share of good organizations flounder for a variety of reasons. Many companies failed because they were operations-driven instead of customer-focused. The corporate graveyard is littered with the remains of companies like Enron, Woolworth, Compaq, E.F. Hutton, MCI WorldCom, PanAm, TWA, Sears Roebuck, and Eastern Airlines, to name but a few. I've witnessed leaders make poor decisions that might have been good for the company's bottom line in the short-term but drove away customers. On the other hand, I've seen leaders guide their companies through rough waters in order to make the transformation from an unconscious company – that is, one that focuses exclusively on revenues and profits at the expense of its employees and customers – to a conscious company – that is, one that leverages its Culture to achieve sound financial results while earning the trust and respect of its employees and the loyal following of its customers. Consider Apple, Google, Amazon, Netflix, 3M, Starbucks and Berkshire Hathaway, to name just a familiar few. These companies are not perfect, but they understand their Culture and leverage it to achieve customer loyalty and strong financial results.

The first step to gaining a better understanding of your Culture is to read The *Heart and Soul of Culture* and then apply its principles and recommendations. I know from the Culture Assessments that our company has performed that once you understand your Culture, you can begin the transformation to a conscious company and achieve great results. As Tom Hinton and Barb Yager tell us in their book, "It's not rocket science, but it does require strong leadership, courage and an unwavering commitment to champion positive change."

Tony Alessandra, Ph.D.

www.alessandra.com
Author of The NEW Art of Managing People and People Smart in Business

Chapter 1
Why Culture Matters and How It Impacts Your Brand and Bottom Line

What is the one factor that significantly distinguishes your business from its competition? While there are many answers to this question – and all have some relevance and application to the success and profitability of your business – after eight years of studying and researching hundreds of companies, nonprofit organizations and government agencies, we have concluded that the number one factor is your *Culture*!

In a nutshell, we have found that *Culture* is what attracts talented employees to your organization and keeps them engaged. Culture is that inexplicable element called energy that attracts customers to your stores or website. Culture is that invisible but transparent factor that creates Broadcast Customers, a strong social media following and, ultimately, profitability.

When we set out to write *The Heart and Soul of Culture*, we struggled with how to explain the "Culture Phenomena." We used our own experiences in the field of consulting, and we studied the most noted research papers on the subject. We also read dozens of business books dating back to Alfred Sloan of General Motors, respected management guru Dr. Peter Drucker, and *In Search of Excellence* author Tom Peters, all of whom discussed successful leadership practices, proven management theories, and the importance of Culture as a contributing factor to a company's growth and success. But frankly, we found very little information on Culture as it relates to a company's long-term profitability; or between Culture and the innovative spirit of its employees; or between Culture and employee engagement; or between Culture and a company's social media image; or between Culture and how it attracts customers; or, finally, between Culture and a company's spiritual or energetic persona.

Let us be very clear. What we discovered from our research and experiences is that Culture and its relevance to your company's profitability and success is not foo-foo. It's not a new-age trend or anything that goes beyond the norm. Culture is quite real, and it impacts your bottom line as well as your top line.

Our challenge in writing this book was to define *Culture* in terms of 21st Century business methods and acceptable practices, and to share with you how to assess your company's Culture and implement a strategy that we refer to as the *Culture Playbook* so your business can compete and succeed in a changing global marketplace. A *Culture Playbook* is a roadmap of your business, a schematic that helps manage culture by applying the Five Ps of Culture to your business. Chapter 14 fully details this important Conscious Business Tool and how it can be used in your business to manage risk.

And so, *The Heart and Soul of Culture* is about two key components of your long-term business success and profitability. First, it's about your Culture and how you define, shape and manage your Culture. Second, and equally important, our book is about helping you make the transition from an unconscious business to a conscious business to save your bottom line. We do this by providing you with several conscious business tools that will help you make that all-important transformation.

We define a conscious business as an entity that embraces the power of its people to achieve its purpose, generate a profit, and inspire, engage and energize its stakeholders. As you ponder this definition, let us pose two questions.

First, *is your market share growing, especially with Millennials and Generation Z customers?* If your answer is anything but a resounding, "Yes!" your business could be in serious trouble! Why? Because these consumers represent the largest emerging consumer market in the world. There are over 100 million of these consumers in the United States alone, and over two billion 16-35-year-old consumers worldwide. Without these customers, your business will struggle to survive. We've heard comments from people who work in government agencies like the Social Security Administration, investment banks and retirement homes tell us, "Our focus is with aging Baby Boomers and consumers over 50." While that continues to be an important market segment, we would argue that focusing your services on such a narrow segment of consumers is flawed because you cannot ignore your customers of tomorrow. If you do, you will lose them to your competition. And, yes, every business and government agency has competition, or will shortly in this changing world of business and politics.

Equally important is knowing what Millennials and Gen Z'ers want and value. The modern currency of Millennials is life experiences. They have accumulated an average per person debt of $42,000 so they're hesitant to buy a new home or car that would plunge them deeper in debt. They live in a society where Likes, swipes and clicks give them instant gratification. Contrast this image with their younger brothers and sisters, Gen Z'ers. This is a generation that MTV refers to as the Founders Generation. This is the generation that considers itself to be agents of change and reform. Gen Z'ers care about equality for all, social justice, the environment and charitable work. They view big companies like Facebook, Wells Fargo, Uber, as well as most politicians, with deep suspicion because of lies, fake news, scandals, deceitful practices, data security breaches and the misuse of their personal information. Ironically, they still do business with most of these big companies. They are also cautious when it comes to a mortgage and taking on more debt because they've witnessed how debt hamstrings their older brothers and sisters.

Both Millennials and Gen Z'ers want more time to enjoy the things they value in life. What they don't want is for businesses to waste their precious time. For example, our research reveals that the under-35-year-old consumers want fast, inexpensive, innovative products and services that work right the first time and don't require costly repairs. They want products that enhance and complement the environment, as well as products and services that bring the world closer together. They want to support companies that honor their words and promises, and they want to be treated fairly and professionally. Also, they want their data protected. Just ask Facebook, Yahoo! or Equifax if data distribution or data piracy matters!

Millennials and Gen Z'ers don't like complexity, duplicity, wasting time or bureaucracy. They'll abide by the rules so long as the rules make sense. In essence, they're looking for products and services that make their life easier and more enjoyable.

When you consider that Millennials currently make up 37% of the workforce, and by 2020 they will represent 46% of the working population, it makes sense to understand their wants and needs. Perhaps the best example of what Millennials want and need comes from Elizabeth McLeod, a millennial and graduate of Boston University who, along with her mother, Lisa Earle McLeod, a speaker and the author of the book, *Selling with Noble Purpose: How to Drive Revenue and Do Work That Makes You Proud*, posted this piece in October 2015. We think it's a real eye-opener and even more relevant today than four years ago.

It's entitled:
An Open Letter to Management:

You hired us thinking this one might be different; and, this one might be in it for the long haul. We're six months in, giving everything we have, then suddenly, we drop a bomb on you. **We're quitting!**

We know the stereotypes. Millennials never settle down. We're drowning in debt for useless degrees. We refuse to put our phone away. We are addicted to lattes even at the expense of our water bill. Our bosses are not wrong about these perceptions. But pointing to our sometimes-irresponsible spending and fear of interpersonal commitment isn't going to solve your problem. You still need us. We're the ones who've mastered social media, who have the energy of a thousand suns, and who will knock back 5-dollar macchiatos until the job is done perfectly.

I've worked in corporate America, administrative offices, advertising agencies, and restaurants. I've had bosses ranging from 24 to 64. I've had bosses I loved, and bosses I didn't. I've seen my peers quit, and I've quit a few times myself. Here's what's really behind your millennials' resignation letter:

1. You tolerate low-performance:

It's downright debilitating to a high achiever. I'm working my heart out, and every time I look up Donna-Do-Nothing is contemplating how long is too long to take for lunch. I start wondering why leadership tolerates this.

Is that the standard here? No thanks.

Fact: Poor performers have a chilling effect on everyone.

2. ROI is not enough for me:

I spent Sunday thinking about how I can make a difference to our customers. Now it's Monday morning, what do I hear? Stock price. Billing. ROI. Suddenly, my Monday power playlist seems useless. I'm sitting in a conference room listening to you drag on about cash flow.

I was making more money bartending in college than I am at this entry-level job. You say I'll get a raise in a year if the company hits a certain number? So what? I need something to care about today. Talk to me about how we make a difference, not your ROI report.

Fact: Organizations with a purpose bigger than money have a growth rate triple that of their competitors.

3. Culture is more than free Panera:

Don't confuse culture with collateral. Yes, I am a cash-strapped millennial who really appreciates free lunch. But I don't wake up at 6AM every day to play foosball in the break room. I'm not inspired to be more innovative over a Bacon Turkey Bravo. I need to be surrounded by people who are on fire for what we're doing. I need a manager who is motivated to push boundaries and think differently.

Working in a cool office is really awesome. So is free lunch. But a purposeful culture is more important.

Fact: A culture of purpose drives exponential sales growth.

4. It's ok to get personal:

Treat me like a number? I'll return the favor. This job will quickly become nothing more than my rent payment. I'll start living for Friday and counting down the minutes until 5. After a few months of that, I'll probably have a drunken epiphany and realize I want more out of my life than this.

Then I'll prove your assumptions right. 8 months in, I'll quit and leave. Or worse, I'll quit and stay, just like Donna-Do-Nothing.

That's not good for either of us. Here's what you need to know:

I was raised to believe I could change the world. I'm desperate for you to show me that the work we do here matters, even just a little bit. I'll make copies, I'll fetch coffee, I'll do the grunt work. But I'm not doing it to help you get a new Mercedes.

I'll give you everything I've got, but I need to know it makes a difference to something bigger than your bottom line.

Signed,
A Millennial

If you're sitting there reading this Open Letter to Management and critiquing the spelling and punctuation (we left it as it was written), you've missed the point! You've hired a talented 20-something who has passion, desire, talent, imagination, and wants to change the world, and your management style or Culture isn't cutting it. In essence, you're being fired! This young Millennial is quitting and taking all her talents and capabilities to your competitor! Chew on that for a while. If that doesn't make you sick to your stomach and get you to start posing some serious questions to your management team, this book won't help you.

The second question is this: *Does your Culture really matter?* We believe it does. Just ask Volkswagen, BP Oil, Takata, Uber, Toyota, the Veterans Administration, FIFA, Yum, Toshiba, Enron, DraftKings, Brazil's state-owned oil giant, Petrobras, Penn State University, Michigan State University, Papa John's Pizza, Wells Fargo, Facebook, and United Airlines. Each of these companies, government agencies, universities and non-profit organizations has seen their brand badly damaged or temporarily tarnished because they strayed from the core tenets and principles that once defined, guided and protected their organizations.

After several years of being relegated to the sideline, Culture is back. Companies, nonprofit organizations, government agencies – and even sports teams – are once again paying attention to the importance of their Culture. More leaders are recognizing that Culture impacts their brands. "Culture eats strategy for breakfast," was a popular phrase in the '80s and '90s, originated by the late management guru, Dr. Peter Drucker, and made famous by Mark Fields, former president of Ford. It's absolutely true! Companies must be careful when developing or refining their strategic plans not to disconnect the two. It's essential that your organization have a healthy Culture if you want to maintain a strong bottom line. We like to tell our audiences that "You can't have a strong bottom line with a weak top line."

We believe that Culture is a "top line" ingredient that must be part of your profitability recipe if you want to create long-term success and a high-performance organization. Let's be clear. Managing your organization's Culture is not an option. There are too many forces that can damage or derail your company's good reputation. Consider the potential negative impact of social media and what one bad Tweet or review on Yelp can do to turn-off thousands of potential customers or make it more difficult for your company to hire good talent. Managing your Culture is a vital priority and competitive advantage in today's global marketplace. Our research reveals that a healthy Culture helps create more satisfied customers and higher levels of employee engagement. This translates to lower employee turnover and absenteeism, fewer safety-related accidents, higher quality, more sales, and higher profits.

How do you maintain Culture coherence, which we define as aligning your brands and goals with the Five Ps of Culture – Purpose, Principles, People, Processes and Performance? There are three factors. First, it starts with leaders making the right decisions and good choices when it comes to developing and protecting their brands and advancing their marketing and sales strategies. The old expression "You can't fix stupid," is also true. When senior leaders make bad decisions or exercise poor judgment, the business and brand will suffer. You cannot undo bad decisions and stupidity on the part of senior leadership without paying a severe price. Look at Uber, Papa John's, Volkswagen, United Airlines, Fox News, BP Oil, Wells Fargo and the Harvey Weinstein Company as examples of what happens when leaders make bad decisions or exercise poor judgment. The company suffers.

Second, we know that your organization's success is contingent upon managing your Culture strategy, just as you would manage your operational strategy. This is why we developed the *Culture Playbook*, a valuable tool we created several years ago to protect our clients' reputation as well as to successfully help them make the transition from an unconscious business to a conscious business.

The *Culture Playbook* should be an important part of every company's strategic plan so we have devoted an entire chapter to it. Ironically, while many companies spend a significant amount of time and money developing their strategic and operational plans, they spend little time thinking about their Culture and how it can be fine-tuned to ensure it is healthy, aligned with their brand, and compliments their strategic and operational plans.

We know that if every disgraced company or government agency listed in the first paragraph of this book – or at least those companies whose leaders had a conscience – had reviewed their *Culture Playbook* before making bad decisions, their companies and organizations might not be listed among the worst scandals of the 21st Century. Unfortunately, the powerful axiom "the more things change, the more they stay the same" is applicable in business because leaders are human, and sometimes leaders do stupid things without thinking through the negative consequences of their decisions. This is why many companies and government agencies continue to make the same dumb mistakes over and over again, and nations continue to fight unwinnable wars. We don't learn from others' mistakes, let alone our own.

You might remember when Culture was a hot topic among CEOs and leading consultants in the 1990s, but it slipped off the radar screen as stock profits soared and the social media craze swept us into the 21st Century. That scenario is repeating itself thirty years later. Today, times are good, but with the advent of social media, smart phones, and whistle-blowers, there are no secrets. Companies can no longer hide their warts and blemishes because every consumer has access to social media, and whistleblowers are rightly rewarded for sounding the alarm on their employers who cheat, lie and misrepresent their products or services to consumers. As Wells Fargo painfully learned, you can't fire 5,000 employees without somebody asking questions and challenging leaders as to what happened and who knew *what*, when.

In 2015, author and speaker Geoffrey James wrote the following about one of the Top 10 Brand Scandals of the Year. The unfortunate company was Books-A-Million, whom James considered the worst offender on his 2015 list.

> "Just 14% of employees said they would recommend this company to a friend. Books-A-Million's culture and value were rated just 1.8, the lowest among companies reviewed. CEO Terry Finley is also not popular, with just 22% thinking he is doing a good job. Over the past several years, the company has struggled to keep up with other large retail and online book sellers like Barnes & Noble and Amazon.com."

While James' interpretation of Culture and values is narrowly focused on the opinions of Books-A-Million's employees and their evaluation of the company's leadership, his point should not be ignored. When your company loses the support and loyalty of its employees, you're finished as a leader. Rarely when a company underperforms and morale collapses, is it the fault of the employees. We've never heard of a baseball or football team firing all its players. That just doesn't happen. Instead, it's the manager or coach who gets the axe. Why? Because leaders are responsible for the success or failings of an organization. They are also responsible – along with the Board of Directors – for their Culture and the success or failure of its brands.

Fortunately, the relevance of Culture is back – front and center – thanks to several important factors. First and foremost, consumers want to know that a company's products or services are not only worthy of their support but, equally important, consumers want to know that your business is putting the customer's interests ahead of profits. This holds true in the non-profit sector as well as in the public sector. As we've noted several times in this book, thanks to social media, there are no secrets. A negative customer experience is blasted across Twitter, Facebook, YouTube, Instagram, Yelp, Trip Advisor or other popular social media websites in nanoseconds. Whether or not the comment or criticism is fair, every customer's comment carries weight.

Also, a growing number of consumers – including an entire generation of Millennials and Gen Z'ers – want to know that your products and services are good for the environment and the planet. A company can no longer hide behind weak excuses, exemptions, apologies or "please give us more time" delay tactics.

Third, auditors and regulators have discovered that a company's Culture is a strong indicator of how your business is meeting its legal obligations. In fact, a company's Culture also has proven to be a reliable indicator of the company's vulnerability in terms of risks, operational challenges, reputation, employee turnover, compliance, and legal entanglements.

At the same time, auditors and regulators are finding that companies operating with a *high-performance Culture* (High Performance Culture is detailed in Chapter 3) have fewer risks and regulatory concerns because they have developed a balance among their business operations, profit strategies and customer relationships.

Another key reason that Culture is back on center stage is the war for talent. Companies are fighting to keep their best-and-brightest employees. One east coast aerospace and defense firm lamented to us that it was losing seasoned engineers to Google and other Silicon Valley companies that were offering higher wages, more employee benefits and the "feel good" lifestyle of northern California or a lower cost-of-living lifestyle in Austin, Texas.

When you consider the triple threat of employee retention, employee engagement and customer relationships, it's no wonder that a company's Culture – and how it impacts employees and customers – is making a strong comeback and once again occupying an important seat in the C-suite. This also explains the rapid growth of Chief Culture Officers who are being hired in the private and public sectors.

The Consequences of Ignoring Culture

Consider the consequences of what happens when companies, agencies, and even churches abandon their Culture by straying from their guiding principles and ignore sacred values that helped build the organization's reputational excellence. We need only look at a handful of businesses that lost their integrity or witnessed the expulsion of their leaders. In some cases, we saw the demise of the entity.

Recently, the sterling reputations of Michigan State University, USA Gymnastics and the U.S. Olympic Committee have been tarnished because of the sexual abuse convictions of one of its sports doctors. Lawrence (Larry) Nassar, who was a team doctor at USA Gymnastics, a nonprofit organization that trains potential Olympians under a charter from the U.S. Olympic Committee, was sentenced to over 100 years in prison in February 2018 for sexually abusing more than 150 female gymnasts who were training under the banner of USA Gymnastics. Nassar, who earned his medical degree from Michigan State University, became a team physician and assistant professor at MSU in 1997. For reasons that have never been explained, Nassar was hired by MSU three years after the first sexual abuse allegations were filed against him. How did that happen? It begs the question – did MSU encourage a Culture of tolerating sexual abuse or at least turn a blind eye to a colleague's inappropriate and illegal sexual behavior?

Whatever caused Michigan State University's actions and cover-up has come at a very steep price since the university agreed to a $500 million settlement with 332 women who sued MSU because of claims they were sexually abused by Larry Nassar.

The Associated Press likened Michigan State University's behavior to Penn State University, where three senior officials, including the school's president, were sentenced to jail in 2017 for failing to tell authorities about a sexual abuse allegation involving assistant football coach Jerry Sandusky.

What's incredible is that many of the more than 150 women and girls who have accused Nassar of sexual assault said they complained to MSU's sports medicine staff, a campus counselor and the women's gymnastics coach as far back as the late 1990s, but nothing was done. Why?

Michigan state law classifies the failure to report sexual assault as a misdemeanor punishable by up to three months in jail and a $500 fine for certain professionals who fail to report a suspected case of child abuse. Lou Anna Simon, who resigned under pressure as Michigan State's president, insisted, "There is no cover-up." But Judge Rosemarie Aquilina called for "a massive investigation as to why there was inaction, why there was silence?"

We have the same questions. What does it say about the Culture of an institution when senior leadership either ignores or fails to report such hideous allegations by a member of their staff, and why has no one in the chain of command at Michigan State or the USA Gymnastics been charged with a crime?

It certainly makes one question the biases of the attorney who oversees criminal prosecution in Ingham County, Michigan where Michigan State University is located. Ironically, Stuart Dunnings III, the elected Ingham County Prosecutor for 16 years (January 1, 1997 – July 2, 2016) was charged with sex-solicitation-related crimes and convicted in August 2016. He was sentenced to a year in prison and three-years of probation. How bizarre is it that the Ingham County prosecutor's office was under the leadership of a sexual deviant while Dr. Larry Nassar was committing his sex crimes at Michigan State University? Is it any wonder that Nassar was never arrested for his sex crimes during this same period?

John Manly, an attorney who represented numerous plaintiffs in the case against Larry Nassar, said of Michigan State University, "They had an opportunity, instead of being another Penn State, to make themselves a beacon of how to handle this. It's too late. You can't fix it now." We agree. When the leadership is rotten at the top, the entire organizational Culture is infected. This is how a bad situation becomes a nightmare and damages the reputation and brand of a business, including universities like Michigan State and Penn State.

No institution is above the law. This rule even applies to venerable institutions like CBS, the giant network that terminated its CEO, Les Moonves amid a flurry of sexual misconduct allegations, and the Catholic Church whose reputation has been riddled and damaged as a result of hundreds of child sex abuse cases at the hands of pedophile priests, nuns and members of other religious orders over the past 60 years. From a Culture perspective, we wonder how a global religious institution could stray so far from its sacred core tenets and principles. The serious nature of the sex abuse accusations, investigations, trials and convictions – not to mention the revelations about attempts to cover-up many of these incidents to protect guilty clergy – has resulted in a staggering settlement of more than one billion dollars so far. Equally important, the scandal has caused a serious decline of worshippers, a significant drop in church attendance and a decline in new converts. So what went wrong?

From our perspective, the Catholic Church had a growing cancer within its clergy, and many bishops and cardinals failed to identify it or confront it until the pedophile problem was so significant that church leaders decided to play two strategies – denial and quiet, out-of-court settlements. Both strategies were not only flawed, but immoral.

When the sex abuse scandal began to receive significant media attention in the 1990s through a series of documentaries and television shows such as Suffer the Children, Deliver Us From Evil, The Boys of St. Vincent and Hands of God, the hierarchy of the Catholic Church could no longer control the storyline or continue to deny the scope of the problem. Then, in 2015, Tom McCarthy's film, Spotlight, a film about The Boston Globe's special investigation team that exposed hundreds of cases of widespread and systemic child sex abuse in the Boston area by numerous priests, won the Academy Award for Best Picture.

This movie rocked the Catholic Church in America and sent a strong message to the Vatican that it needed to address and fix a problem. Internal investigations and public records showed that more than 3,000 priests had been involved in sexual abuse cases dating back some 60 years.

From a Culture viewpoint, our experience tells us that it will be very difficult for a global institution like the Catholic Church to make the necessary changes without undergoing a major reformation. These changes need to address the marital status of clergy, celibacy and homosexuality among priests and nuns, the declining number of men entering the priesthood, and the requirement for screening priests for healthy psycho-sexual development. Trying to reach consensus on any one of these topics, let alone bring them to the forefront for discussion among church leaders, is nearly impossible.

Again, from a Culture perspective, we cite this example of the Catholic Church's child sex abuse problems to demonstrate how difficult it is for any institution to change its ways, despite having a very clear charter and strong guiding principles to steer it through challenging times. Sometimes it's not enough for leaders to accept responsibility for the misdeeds of its employees and try to square things with the thousands of sexually abused victims through cash settlements. When the cancer has spread so deeply into the corpus of the organization, it cannot survive in its present form. Despite feeble attempts by senior Vatican officials, the core problem has not been solved and cannot be solved by apologies and throwing money at sex abuse victims.

Until a Culture assessment is conducted and the results of that assessment are fully implemented, we believe these kinds of problems will persist for the Church, and membership and support will continue to decline.

At the other end of the spectrum is how the University of Maryland's president, Wallace Loh, addressed the tragic death of Jordan McNair, a 19-year-old football player who collapsed following a strenuous spring training practice. McNair, a sophomore, died two weeks after collapsing from heatstroke during football practice on May 29, 2018. He reportedly had a temperature of 106 degrees Fahrenheit and was hospitalized following the incident, but a McNair family attorney said the team personnel was slow to seek medical attention. According to ESPN, they waited an hour after the offensive lineman suffered a seizure before calling 9-1-1.

In addressing the tragedy, President Loh did not skirt the university's responsibility, nor did he place the blame on anyone outside the school's athletic training staff. Loh apologized to the McNair family and stated publicly that the University of Maryland accepted moral responsibility for its training staff mistakes that led to McNair's death several weeks after he collapsed.

Loh told the media, "I wanted the McNair family to hear it directly from me this morning – the university accepts legal and moral responsibility for the mistakes that our training staff made on that fateful workout day of May the 29th, which, of course, led subsequently to his death on June 13, 2018."

"The university owes you an apology. You entrusted Jordan to our care and he is never returning home again," he told McNair's parents. During a news conference, Loh said that some of the university's policies and protocols "do not conform to best practices." Loh added that ultimately the athletic training staff "basically misdiagnosed the situation." According to the preliminary reports from an ongoing investigation launched by the university, no vital signs were taken and "other safeguards that should have been taken were not."

Maryland's athletic director, Damon Evans, revealed that the athletic training staff failed to take McNair's temperature following his seizure and did not apply a cold-water immersion treatment. The athletic trainer, who was reportedly leading McNair's final conditioning workout, resigned following the tragedy. Also, the university's head football coach, DJ Durkin, was placed on a two-month administrative leave until the university completed its internal investigation. It was during this period that ESPN issued a critical report detailing a "culture of humiliation and intimidation inside the Maryland (football) program." When Durkin was reinstated by the university's Board of Regents, there was an uproar of protests and the university's president stepped in and fired the football coach.

What Maryland's President Loh said and did strikes us as role model behavior for a leader. Instead of hiding behind lawyers and allowing a difficult situation to play out in a lawsuit that the university would most likely lose, President Loh took the high road and accepted blame and responsibility for his university's failure to do everything it could have and should have done to ensure McNair's safety. Loh also acknowledged that the university might have Culture problems in terms of how hard it pushed its athletes. From our perspective, this is how a conscious leader acts and responds when faced with a difficult and tragic situation. The conscious leader steps forward, acknowledges the problem, accepts responsibility, and pledges to fix it, then he/she does exactly that. This is how a Culture-driven organization behaves in the face of adversity or crisis.

Some in the media criticized the university's response as "too little, too late" because it came 63 days after McNair's death. Several critics asked the damning question, "How does a self-described global educational leader like the University of Maryland fail to have leadership in place that puts the well-being of the people with whom it's entrusted above all else?" It's a fair question and one that every university athletic program should ponder. The obvious answer in this case is the head football coach is responsible for his staff and players. When they fail, it's the coach who is held responsible, and rightly so. This is why the University of Maryland suspended, and ultimately had to fire, their head football coach.

President Loh's news conference came four days after ESPN published a searing report about the Culture of the Maryland football program. However, from our perspective, we understand that such incidents and tragedies take time to properly investigate. Unfortunately, investigations never move fast enough for the media and public. Putting together the pieces of what happened and who did what when takes time. Of course, allowing an athlete to die simply because basic medical procedures were either ignored or not in place is inexcusable. And from a Culture perspective, every university should be reviewing both its principles and processes as they relate to the treatment of student-athletes when fatigue, heat exhaustion and other medical issues occur.

Ohio State University was forced to act when it was revealed that its head football coach, Urban Meyer, mishandled domestic assault accusations made against one of his assistant coaches who was later terminated. Although Coach Meyer was made aware of the domestic abuse accusations and reported them to the university's athletic director, no further action was taken by either Coach Meyer or Gene Smith, OSU's athletic director. When more domestic assault accusations were filed by the assistant coach's wife, it became front-page news in the media and OSU was forced to investigate. Coach Meyer was suspended for the team's first three games of the 2018 football season, and OSU athletic director Gene Smith was suspended without pay for three weeks. At the end of the 2018 football season, Coach Meyer announced his retirement.

In a public statement, OSU said, "Although neither Urban Meyer nor Gene Smith condoned or covered-up the alleged domestic abuse by Assistant Coach Zach Smith, they failed to take sufficient management action relating to Zach Smith's misconduct and retained an assistant coach who was not performing as an appropriate role model for OSU student-athletes."

At the heart of OSU's well-crafted statement is the Culture-based language "appropriate role model for OSU student-athletes." Regardless of whether or not OSU was forced to take action against their popular coach and athletic director as a result of public pressure and the media frenzy, the university acted in concert with its core principles. The university also acted quickly and decisively to get ahead of the negative publicity and control any further negative fallout from this unpleasant situation, including loss of reputation.

In the case of Facebook, the popular social media giant, the question is not so much about competency of its leadership but rather a matter of how principles and processes were ignored and neglected for profits and favoritism. Facebook's policy of sharing user data caused a firestorm within Facebook, resulting in the loss of millions of dollars in advertising revenue and hundreds of thousands of disenfranchised Facebook customers who closed their accounts.

What happened? While the jury is still out as this saga unfolds, it's a story of political intrigue and preferential treatment for 61 firms, including a company, Cambridge Analytica, founded by Donald Trump's former campaign operative and advisor, Steve Bannon. Ultimately, it's a story about a lack of integrity on the part of Facebook's senior leadership and omissions by those same leaders who were less than honest with its 50 million users whose data was sold, misused and compromised.

Here are the facts as reported by numerous media outlets: Facebook exposed data on more than 50 million Facebook users to a researcher who worked at Cambridge Analytica. Cambridge Analytica was created when Steve Bannon approached conservative mega-donors, Rebekah and Robert Mercer, to fund a political consulting firm. Bannon became vice president of the firm, and during the 2016 election, he reached out to the Trump campaign to introduce them to Cambridge Analytica. A third party, SLC Group, an international public relations and messaging firm that specializes in influence operations for political campaigns, was contracted by Cambridge Analytica to perform services on behalf of the Trump campaign. During this process, the firm used a researcher, Aleksandr Kogan, a Russian-American, to build a Facebook app that was a quiz. This app not only collected data from people who took the quiz, but it also exposed a loophole within Facebook that allowed the app to collect data from Facebook users, as well as friends of the quiz takers.

When Facebook learned of the breach, it prohibited the selling of data collected using this method, but Cambridge Analytica ignored the restrictions and sold the data anyway. Facebook CEO Mark Zuckerberg found himself and his company in the awkward position of being both a victim of data piracy and a co-conspirator in the act of having violated its pledge to protect the data of Facebook customers.

In response to the scandal, Zuckerberg wrote, "I've been working to understand exactly what happened and how to make sure this doesn't happen again. The good news is that the most important actions to prevent this from happening again today we have already taken years ago. But we also made mistakes, there's more to do, and we need to step up and do it."

The story doesn't end there because Facebook later disclosed more disturbing facts after the Wall Street Journal revealed that Facebook had special deals with 61 app developers, device and software makers that gave these app developers time to become compliant with changes in Facebook's policies, and to enable device and software makers to create versions of the social network for their products. Facebook disclosed that it was still sharing information of users' friends such as their name, gender, birthday, residency, photos and Page Likes. This revelation came six months after Facebook said it had stopped access to this data in 2015 and walled off any further access by preferred app developers or vendors. Why the double talk? It makes us wonder who's in charge of protecting Facebook's reputation and cultural integrity, and does Facebook really care about data piracy or is the company strictly profit-driven? These are serious questions that a conscious business would want to answer truthfully and immediately correct any malpractice.

As we go to press, Facebook has faced congressional hearings and dozens of lawsuits from its users and several state attorneys general for data piracy. Also, numerous Facebook employees have expressed their concern about how the company prioritizes user protection – if, at all – in its decision-making process. Apparently, there is mounting tension between Facebook's data security team and its legal team in terms of deciding how to best protect user data. The bottom line to this internal challenge is protecting data versus making more money for the company.

To make matters worse, on Thursday, July 26, 2018, Facebook lost nearly $120 billion in market capitalization when its earnings report revealed the company would miss expectations on revenue for 2018. To complicate matters, the company reported slowing user growth. Investors were also rattled by what they described as weak leadership guidance. Incredibly, the social media behemoth's stock lost roughly one-fifth of its value in a single trading session. Facebook's stock closed down 19%, which erased all the company's 2018 gains. Its market capitalization dropped in a single day from $630 billion to $510 billion. This was the worst single-session decline in the history of Wall Street trading and the ugliest single-session decline since Facebook went public in 2012. This is what can happen to a well-respected company when leaders ignore their Culture and make poor decisions. As of March 15, 2018, Facebook's stock was priced at $165 per share and its valuation is over $436 billion.

More recently, a USA Today report printed on December 5, 2018 indicated that Mark Zuckerberg had written a chain of emails that "aggressively hunted for ways to make money from the reams of personal information Facebook was collecting from users." While there's no indication that Facebook went forward with a proposal to charge app developers for access to the personal information of Facebook users, it raises a serious Culture question for us: *Is Facebook putting profits ahead of its sacred responsibility to protect its users' data?*

While the struggle between profits and protecting users' data is not an uncommon struggle facing many tech companies, in the case of Facebook, when issues like this blow-up and cause serious damage to its reputational leadership and bottom line, the Monday morning quarterbacks quickly say, "I told you so!" but the deeper issue here is about trust. Can users trust Facebook with their personal data, and is Facebook in violation of their own User Agreement?

When people begin to question a company's credibility, they start to ask serious questions such as how could one third-party developer create an app that would exploit and circumvent the many safeguards Facebook had in place to protect its users' data? Also, how does Facebook select its partners and suppliers? Was Cambridge Analytica properly vetted by Facebook or did fast money outweigh the company's ethics and privacy policies? The final question, and the most serious, is how could Facebook not have known this scenario was happening shortly after the data transfer (or before) and do nothing to stop it?

As one reporter suggested, "It would be one thing if this were a new, one-time error. But Facebook has known about this for more than two years, and only now are they actually acknowledging they made a mistake."

We go to print without knowing how this saga of distrust and deceit will play out for Facebook, but we do know that Facebook must address several issues that relate to its Culture. This is the reason for several television commercials launched by Facebook that focus on trust and the reliability of its brand, although public relations campaigns cannot fix everything. Among those issues are: trust, data piracy, broken processes, broken promises to consumers, the selection of its suppliers and partners, and managing its third-party developers. Finally, Facebook's senior leadership must recognize its responsibility in advancing the cause of safeguarding data as social media continues to play a significant role in how we communicate and do business on a global basis.

A "nightmare" is how some senior medical officers described conditions at the United States Army's Walter Reed Army Medical Center in Washington, D.C. in 2004. This is when a series of allegations were raised about unsatisfactory, putrid living conditions for wounded soldiers. Allegations were also raised about the mistreatment of military patients and the dilapidated facilities that housed these heroes. This once-proud medical facility, which treated soldiers suffering from traumatic brain injuries, amputations, and stress disorders, was severely criticized by several newspaper reporters for its patient neglect and shoddy living conditions.

Perhaps it's helpful to recall why the Department of Veterans Affairs (VA) was created in the first place. Its roots can be traced back to 1636 when the Pilgrims of Plymouth Colony were at war with the Pequot Indians. The Pilgrims passed a law that stated that disabled soldiers would be supported by the colony. In 1864, President Abraham Lincoln clarified the mission of the Veterans Bureau when he declared in his Second Inaugural Address that it was the nation's responsibility "To care for him who shall have borne the battle, and for his widow, and his orphan..." In 1930, President Hoover signed Executive Order 5398 and elevated the Veterans Bureau to a federal administration – creating the Veterans Administration – to "consolidate and coordinate Government activities affecting war veterans." At that time, the National Homes and Pension Bureau also joined the VA. We share this with you because it's important to understand how an organization's Culture evolves over time, and yet its proud mission remained unchanged after 150 years. What did change was its leadership and how the VA's leaders – both in Washington, D.C. and at the regional level – failed to fulfill the VA's mission.

The Washington Post reported that "Soldiers suffering from traumatic brain injuries or stress disorders, others with amputated limbs, have languished for weeks and months on end in vermin-infested quarters waiting for a decision on their military status and a ruling on the level of benefits they will receive if they are discharged and transferred to the civilian-run Veterans Administration (VA) healthcare system."

When the scandal broke, it was reported that soldiers were pressured to keep quiet and even punished with daily inspections if they dared speak to the media. Significant public and media attention were generated which, in turn, prompted numerous congressional and executive actions, including the resignations of several high-ranking military officers at Walter Reed Army Medical Center and, eventually, the closing of the original facility in northwest Washington, D.C.

A few years later, the National Naval Medical Center and Walter Reed Army Medical Center (WRNMMC) were joined together in September 2011 to form Walter Reed National Military Medical Center as decreed by the Base Realignment and Closure law of 2005. Today, WRNMMC is comprised of nearly 8,500 medical professionals and support staff who serve military families and America's active duty, returning war heroes, veterans and leaders. The Vision of WRNMMC is the following:

We are committed to operational readiness; outstanding customer service; maintaining excellent graduate medical and dental education and research; and always delivering world-class health care within an integrated system. Those who come through our doors, come to heal, to stay healthy, to help others, to teach the next generation, to practice quality medicine, and take part in cutting-edge clinical research.

This vision is a complete reversal from the old way wounded soldiers were once treated. In fact, the public outcry was so strong that private citizens like Arnold Fisher, the successful New York City developer and president of Fisher Brothers, stepped in and established the Intrepid Fallen Heroes Fund, which has raised nearly $200 million and is constructing nine special traumatic brain injury treatment facilities on military bases across the country. Fisher named these centers Intrepid Spirit Centers, named after the World War II aircraft carrier, Intrepid, that he rescued from the scrapyard and now serves as a living museum and the home of Fleet Week in New York City's Hudson River. Each Intrepid Spirit Center is approximately 25,000 square feet and costs approximately $11 million to build and equip. While much of the operation at these centers involves research for traumatic brain injuries and psychological health conditions, Intrepid Spirit care also focuses on diagnosis and treatment.

This is an example of Culture at its best – private citizens taking responsibility to get the job done and doing the right thing when those who were charged with the welfare of our soldiers failed in their mission because of misguided leadership, bureaucratic red tape, or trying to manipulate the system for their own selfish gain or "cover-your-ass" tactics.

WRNMMC claims it's moving toward a new horizon in health care – one that offers "synergy and revolutionary collaboration." In our research, we have seen first-hand evidence that medical care for America's soldiers and sailors at the WRNMMC has dramatically improved as a result of new policies, procedures and refinements to its Culture that was created by seasoned physicians and capable leaders from the highly respected Medical Corps of the United States Navy, which has been integrated into the chain-of-command and valued for its expertise and distinguished medical performance for nearly 200 years.

Our review also suggests that the Walter Reed Medical Center scenario was not an isolated incident. Rather, it stemmed from a flawed Army medical Culture that placed the needs and selfish interests of senior officers and management ahead of its stakeholders – the wounded warriors who valiantly served our nation. In a *balanced Culture*, or even an *under-performing Culture*, mistakes are acknowledged and eventually fixed. But in a *volatile Culture*, mistakes are compounded, whistleblowers are punished, and management considers itself to be infallible. This is why Walter Reed Hospital failed under the U.S. Army's inept leadership.

As further proof of a *volatile Culture* within the ranks of the Army's Medical Corps during this troubling period, there were numerous other abuses, mismanagement and related embarrassments reported. As one senior Army officer told us, "It was as if a 'MASH' mentality prevailed within the Army's Medical

Corps from the top down. Nobody at the top gave a shit about the soldiers who just wanted good medical care. So why bother? It was depressing."

Similar experiences about the Veterans Administration's flawed Culture were shared with us. In 2014, less than ten years after the Walter Reed Army Medical Center scandal broke, similar abuses and charges were discovered at the Veterans Administration.

Senior managers at several VA centers altered actual appointment schedules to minimize delays in treating over 120,000 veterans. Unfortunately, this was just the tip of the iceberg as thousands of veterans endured delays due to their inability to get appointments for serious medical conditions. That same year, CNN reported that at least 40 United States Armed Forces veterans died while waiting for urgent medical care at the Phoenix Veterans Health Administration facilities. In May 2014, the Veterans Health Administration's top health official, Dr. Robert Petzel, retired early at the request of Secretary of Veterans Affairs Eric Shinseki.

Two weeks later, Secretary Shinseki resigned amid the fallout from the controversy which was expanded to include several other VA medical centers around the nation with the same mismanagement problems as the Phoenix facility.

How do organizations – entrusted with sacred missions – stray so far from their core values and principles? At the Veterans Administration, this was not an isolated incident but rather the result of a toxic, top-down, corrupt Culture that had been fermenting for years in several VA centers. Management stopped listening and caring. It's almost that simple.

Instead of honoring the hallowed principles and values upon which the Veterans Administration was established in 1864 and formalized in 1930, a number of managers and leaders, who lacked the courage and fortitude to address major problems and champion the needs of America's veterans, cowered in their responsibilities and allowed a toxic Culture to corrupt this once-proud agency. The results were telling. Front-line employees were pitted against supervisors and, in turn, supervisors were squeezed by management to cut costs and manipulate patient treatment records. Ultimately, quality care began to suffer, and beloved veterans died from neglect.

When an organization asks its people to bend the rules, ignore quality practices and abandon their commitment to the customer, bad things happen. This is what happened at the Veterans Administration over several decades. It was evident from the accounts of well-intentioned employees who were punished or reassigned when they attempted to challenge certain practices that clearly violated honored policies and traditions at the VA.

A Culture that punishes whistleblowers for reporting flawed practices is toxic. When management allows the truth to be suppressed, it is a clear indication that leadership is more concerned about sweeping problems under the carpet instead of fixing what is broken. Such leaders are unworthy to hold their posts. If unchecked by a higher authority, they will bring down the organization. This is what happened to the leadership at the VA.

While those leaders at Walter Reed Army Medical Center and the Veterans Administration were dismissed for their ineptness and disservice to veterans, the question must be asked, "Has the problem been fixed?" The only way to answer that question is to examine the current Culture of those organizations. What is most disturbing to us is the musical chairs atmosphere that has been occurring in the secretary's office. Fired Veterans Affairs Secretary David Shulkin, who was appointed by President Obama, told NPR's Morning Edition that political forces in the Trump administration want to privatize the VA and that he was standing in the way. Shulkin opposed privatization and suggested he was muzzled by the Trump Administration so he could not oppose privatization.

During his confirmation hearing in 2017, former VA secretary Shulkin promised to lead a "major reform and transformation of the VA." Shulkin said he wanted veterans to be able to get care in the private sector when they need it, but he also wanted to maintain core VA services. "There will be far greater accountability, dramatically improved access, responsiveness and expanded care options," he said.

The topic of privatization of the Veterans Administration's healthcare system has been a major issue among politicians in Washington, D.C. for the past few years since the VA crisis first surfaced. While we understand that politics will always influence the thinking and decision-making process within the VA, it's unfortunate that veterans are getting a raw deal from both political parties while the Culture crisis continues.

It's too early to tell if the Culture seeds planted by fresh leadership at the Veterans Administration will bear fruit; hopefully its new leader, Robert Wilkie, who was nominated by President Trump to serve as the tenth Secretary of Veterans Affairs, is a positive step in the direction of creating a Culture of caring.

At Walter Reed Army Medical Center, ten years have passed since its scandal. The old regime is gone and so is the old Walter Reed. Today, that broken Culture has been replaced, as we noted earlier, by a more competent U.S. Navy Medical Corp leadership that is patient-focused and determined to restore military medicine to its lofty place. To do anything less will result in the failure of the entire military medicine system. Much is at stake.

If military medicine's current leaders are not successful in fostering a Culture of excellence in the workplace, many of the capable military physicians, nurses and staff will retire, resign or transfer their talents and skills to the private sector. If this happens, the depletion of these skilled workers will be to the detriment of military medicine and those American warriors who deserve only the best for their years of service. You can now see how important creating a Culture of excellence and pride is to an organization and its people.

What causes seasoned administrators and professionals – including doctors and nurses who took oaths to protect lives and care for their patients – to completely disregard ethical boundaries and fabricate schedules and appointment books? While this is a case of a dysfunctional management system that created the problem, it's their corrupt Culture that created the explosion!

While government agencies have their share of dysfunction, antiquated policies and Culture problems, they are not alone. We need only turn back the clock to April 20, 2010, the day the BP Oil disaster occurred in the Gulf of Mexico. The Deepwater Horizon oil spill, as it became known and popularized by the 2016 blockbuster movie starring Mark Wahlberg and Kate Hudson, was the largest accidental marine oil spill in the history of the petroleum industry. It was an estimated 8% to 31% larger in volume than the previously largest oil spill – the Ixtoc 1 that occurred on June 3, 1979 in the Gulf of Mexico some 62 miles northwest of Ciudad del Carmen.

BP Oil's Deepwater Horizon spill resulted in the deaths of 11 people and discharged an estimated 210 million gallons of oil into pristine Gulf waters, contaminating hundreds of miles of U.S. coastal shorelines and beaches, and devastating the livelihood of hundreds of thousands of residents and businesses along the Gulf of Mexico. The pervasive damage to wildlife and the environment continues today.

Was this simply an offshore oil rig accident? Or was there a deeper problem within BP Oil – one that was rooted in a Culture that was so profit-driven that managers were pressured to disregard safety rules and, in doing so, jeopardized the lives of fellow employees? Upon reviewing public documents, congressional testimony, court records and interviews from BP Oil employees and industry experts, we believe this accident was triggered by a Culture of greed and complete disregard for its employees' safety and the environment. Furthermore, it was encouraged by bad management decisions and disconnected leadership.

While no amount of money can justify the loss of human life and the environmental damage caused by BP Oil's disregard for safety, in November 2012, BP and the U.S. Department of Justice settled federal criminal charges. BP Oil pleaded guilty to 11 counts of manslaughter, two misdemeanors and one felony count of lying to Congress. BP also agreed to four years of government monitoring of its safety practices and ethics. Also, the Environmental Protection Agency announced that BP would be temporarily banned from new contracts with the U.S. government. BP and the Department of Justice agreed to a record-setting $4.525 billion in fines and other payments. From our perspective, the bigger issue is this: has BP Oil changed from an unconscious business to a conscious business? Second, has BP Oil embraced a Culture that allows managers to listen to employees, solicit feedback, pay attention to warning signs and fix minor problems before they erupt into catastrophic disasters? If you believe their advertising campaign and public relations initiative, the answer is "they're trying."

Then we have the ongoing saga of the Takata Corporation, a Japanese company with a successful history dating back to its founding in 1933. When you read the company's promotional literature, you would think this is an honorable company founded on a Culture of excellence:

Takata has been engineering the precision of our products to the millisecond for over 70 years. We have been driven by our dedication to save human life while embracing a pioneering spirit in developing innovative products. Takata has spread this same thought process to all of our locations worldwide. Somewhere on earth, Takata products have saved the preciousness of human life today. We continue to challenge ourselves and our affiliates all over the world to develop new technologies so that people will be able to experience the joy of life. Our dream is that someday there will be zero victims due to traffic accidents. And we hope the day will come when the word "TAKATA" becomes synonymous with "safety."

How ironic that Takata, a company name that should be synonymous with safety, has now become synonymous with death and injury as a result of its faulty auto airbags. Its reputation is now the opposite of those sacred principles upon which the company was founded.

As we examine Takata's history over the past twenty years, we discovered something very troubling. The company that was founded in 1933 on the principles of engineering precision, safety and technologies that save human lives, has become a company fraught with internal problems and a Culture of greed. This is clearly a problem that can only be blamed on bad leadership.

Regrettably, the Takata airbag incident wasn't the company's first negative encounter with regulators and disgruntled consumers. In May 1995, a recall began in the United States affecting 8,428,402 predominantly Japanese vehicles made from 1986 to 1991 with seatbelts manufactured by the Takata Corporation of Japan. At the time, it was the second largest recall in the 30-year history of the U.S. Department of Transportation (DOT). The recall was prompted by an investigation carried out by the National Highway Traffic

Safety Administration (NHTSA) on Takata-equipped Honda vehicles after many of their owners complained of seatbelt buckles either failing to latch, latching and releasing automatically, or releasing in accidents. It revealed that potentially faulty Takata seatbelts were not limited to only Honda vehicles but to other Japanese imports as well. NHTSA launched a second investigation on Takata seatbelts, as well as individual investigations on other vehicle manufacturers using Takata seatbelts, to determine the magnitude of the defect.

Takata originally produced parachutes and other textiles. In the early 1950s, the company entered the seatbelt market, first as a research company, then in the 1960s manufacturing and selling seatbelts. It was Takata that built the world's first crash test plant for testing seatbelts under actual driving conditions.

In 1988, Takata began making airbags. At the time of the recall, Takata had twenty percent of the world market for airbags. But studies show that problems began with Takata airbags around 2004 when 30 injuries and two deaths in the United States related to Takata airbags were first reported.

Takata is now responsible for the largest auto recall in history. Over 47 million autos built by 19 automakers have been recalled because of potentially faulty Takata airbags. At least 22 people worldwide have been killed and hundreds more permanently disfigured when the faulty air bags that deployed exploded and sprayed shrapnel. As one U.S. government official stated in explaining the recall, "Vehicles with Takata airbags could explode and potentially send shrapnel into the face and body of both the driver and front seat passenger. The worst among the defective air bags are known as Alphas, driver-side airbags installed in Hondas that have up to a 50% chance of exploding on impact."

In June 2014, Takata admitted that their Mexican subsidiary, TK Holdings, had mishandled the manufacturing of explosive propellants and improperly stored chemicals used in airbags. Takata's troubles deepened when it became apparent that identifying vehicles with defective airbags would be made more difficult by the failure of its Mexican subsidiary to keep proper quality control records. That prompted another round of recalls by auto companies and the NHTSA in June 2013.

Our examination of Takata suggests the company's problems extend far beyond poor quality control and manufacturing practices. We believe that Takata has serious Culture problems. This is very troubling considering the pride most Japanese companies take in shaping their reputation and creating a Culture of excellence, including Takata when it was founded in 1933.

As we studied Takata's mission and values it became apparent that senior management had drifted away from upholding its core values and principles. When senior management stopped emphasizing the core values upon which Takata was founded, site managers began to apply their own standards, processes and values in place of the cherished values and principles upon which Takata was built. In turn, front-line employees began to disregard high quality standards and ignored good recordkeeping methods, and it failed to document the reporting of manufacturing problems, including the improper storage of the chemicals used in airbags.

As a singular event in a long chain of quality control methods and processes used by a major company, one would not think that poor recordkeeping or the lack of documenting the storage of certain chemicals would be a big deal. However, when you compound these mistakes and inattention to detail by adding them to other key steps in the manufacturing of airbags, bad things can happen. This explains in part why Takata airbags exploded into the faces of unsuspecting drivers and passengers and, in several cases, killed Takata customers.

As one auto company's Chief Culture Officer told us, "When plant managers and frontline employees begin to ignore proven quality standards and fail to enforce the basic processes for the safekeeping of key chemicals and materials, the results will not be good. Too often, sidestepping your quality control processes results in major recalls and, unfortunately for Takata, serious litigation issues – not to mention blood on its hands because people died needlessly."

Finally, how do we even begin to explain why nearly 5,000 Wells Fargo employees conspired to perpetrate a major fraud by submitting fake applications for 565,443 credit card accounts without the consent of its customers? And it appears that number may grow into the millions of falsified accounts by the time the investigation is completed.

How does Wells Fargo explain that nearly 14,000 of these fake accounts incurred more than $400,000 in fees according to CNNMoney? Wells Fargo's illegal actions resulted in a $185 million fine from regulators and the firing of 5,300 employees. What goes wrong within the Culture of a company that allows this criminal behavior to happen? Should the senior executives pay the ultimate price – get fired and go to jail – for their actions?

There's an old Russian proverb, "A fish stinks from the head down." At Wells Fargo, this proverb proved true in 2017. The bank's embattled CEO, John Stumpf, was forced to resign from one of the most powerful and prestigious leadership posts in the banking industry because the fake accounts scandal could not be contained. Senator Elizabeth Warren (D-MA) condemned Stumpf for his "gutless" leadership during a Senate hearing on the matter. CNNMoney reported that while Mr. Stumpf said he was "deeply sorry" and insisted there was no scheme to scam customers, he struggled at times to answer lawmakers' questions. He often gave the impression he wasn't fully aware of what was going on within his own company.

CNNMoney quoted Jeffrey Sonnenfeld, an authority on corporate governance at Yale University, who said, "Stumpf proved to be a deer caught in the headlights with a tin ear in understanding, addressing, and communicating the problem."

Ironically, Stumpf prided himself on Wells Fargo's work ethic. In a 2015 Fortune interview he called himself the "keeper of our company's culture." Unfortunately for Mr. Stumpf, his inability to lead in times of crisis cost him $69 million in compensation and severance, which he forfeited at the request of the Wells Fargo board of directors.

The question must be asked, "How did Mr. Stumpf not know that his retail division was creating fake accounts over a ten-year period?" Did nobody in a leadership position bring this to Mr. Stumpf's attention? Did no one at the bank challenge Carrie Tolstedt, who headed the community banking division at Wells Fargo during the scandal? The C-suite had to know what was going on or they were completely out of touch with the daily operations of the banking giant. Or was it a simple case of incompetent leadership? But wait, there's more!

Carrie Tolstedt lost $19 million in compensation and was forced to resign. Four other senior executives at the bank, also found to be at fault for allowing the deceptive practices to flourish, were fired.

What strikes us as a more deeply-rooted problem within the Wells Fargo Culture is the fact that Wells Fargo fired a number of whistleblowers who tried to report the unethical and illegal fake account practices early on by calling the bank's ethics hotline to report the improper sales tactics. This is clearly a sign of a broken Culture that encourages illicit behavior and punishes those who try to protect the brand.

Several former Wells Fargo employees told CNNMoney it was precisely the bank's pressure-cooker sales environment that spurred staffers to open thousands of fake accounts. They were pressured to perform or faced being terminated. No wonder over 5,000 employees cheated bank customers.

In the end, Wells Fargo's corrupt leadership and bad decision-making cost the bank $185 million in fines from the federal government. Several states, including California and Illinois, placed sanctions on Wells Fargo and suspended it from doing business with the state. The suspension caused California's state treasurer, John Chiang, to announce that he would not use the bank as a broker-dealer for investments by the state treasurer's office. Wells Fargo will be banned from underwriting the sale of California bonds, and Treasurer Chiang's office will not purchase more Wells Fargo stocks and bonds beyond what it already owns.

So one must ask the obvious questions: First, when did Wells Fargo's senior leaders learn about the scam to create two million false accounts? Second, did they weigh the consequences of what would happen if they were caught? Third, why did no one in an executive position step-in and stop the illegal and brainless scheme? Finally, where was the bank's Culture and ethics officer during this fiasco?

This is why Culture Officers are an important part of every major company's C-suite. Somebody must be the keeper of the corporate ethics and Culture to prevent the company from making boneheaded decisions and protect employees when they try to stop unethical behavior in an effort to preserve the company's brand reputation.

A unique case that defies all logic relating to values, morals and protecting a proud brand is the saga that has befallen Penn State University, once a university with impeccable credentials, that now has a tarnished reputation as a result of two criminal cases during the past ten years.

The first negative case is often referred to as the Penn State University Sandusky Sex Abuse Scandal. It involved a former defensive football coach, Jerry Sandusky, who worked at Penn State for 32 years under head football coach Joe Paterno. According to news accounts, the sex abuse scandal broke in early November 2011 when Sandusky was indicted on 52 counts of child molestation. Although Sandusky's abuse may have begun in the 1970s, according to several victims who testified in court, he was charged with sex abuse that occurred between 1994 and 2009.

Additionally, three school officials – PSU President Graham Spanier, university Vice President Gary Schultz, and Athletic Director Tim Curley – were charged with perjury, obstruction of justice, failure to report suspected child abuse, and related charges. Shortly after the scandal broke, Mr. Spanier resigned as president. The Penn State University Board of Trustees terminated the contracts of Mr. Curley and football coach, Joe Paterno.

On June 22, 2012, Sandusky was convicted of 45 counts of sexual abuse and was sentenced on October 9, 2012, to a minimum of 30 years and a maximum of 60 years in prison.

It was announced in June 2017 that Graham Spanier was sentenced to 4-12 months in jail for his role and inaction in the Sandusky sex abuse scandal. Tim Curley, 63, received a sentence of 7 to 23 months in prison, and Gary Schultz, 67, was sentenced to a prison term of 6 to 23 months.

When sentencing the three former PSU officials, Judge John Boccabella raised several questions. Interestingly, these are the same questions we would expect every leader to ask under similar circumstances, but in the case of Penn State, nobody bothered to accept responsibility for Sandusky's criminal acts. We can only surmise that PSU's leaders supported a corrupt Culture that protected guilty persons while victims were ignored. Judge Boccabella wondered aloud, "Why Mr. Sandusky was allowed to continue to access the Penn State facilities is beyond me." The judge added, "All three [of you guilty persons] ignored the opportunity to put an end to (Sandusky's) crimes when you had a chance to do so."

The judge also criticized the actions of the late head football coach, Joe Paterno who, like the other administrators, failed to alert child-welfare authorities or police to the 2001 complaint, although he was never charged with a crime. Judge Boccabella said of Paterno, "He could have made that phone call without so much as getting his hands dirty. Why he didn't is beyond me." We would echo the judge's sentiments. It's unfortunate that Coach Paterno's legacy is not about his 409 wins, 136 losses and 3 ties. Instead, his legacy is tainted because – according to an independent investigation initiated by PSU and conducted by former FBI director Louis Freeh – in 2001 Coach Paterno concealed facts relating to Sandusky's sexual abuse of young boys and he may have tried to persuade PSU officials not to report Mr. Sandusky to law enforcement officials.

To complicate matters for Penn State University, Jeffrey Sandusky, the son of former Penn State assistant football coach Jerry Sandusky, was arrested in May 2017 and charged with sexually assaulting two minors according to the complaint obtained by USA TODAY Sports. Pennsylvania State Police detained Sandusky on 14 felony counts involving two girls, including solicitation of statutory sexual assault, solicitation of involuntary deviate sexual intercourse, six counts of unlawful contact with a minor, and two counts each of solicitation to photograph or depict sexual acts, sexual abuse of children and corruption of minors.

Just when Penn State University was trying to put the ugly Sandusky sex abuse scandal behind it, Sandusky's son was arrested and charged with sex abuse crimes.

Then, to compound matters for Penn State University, a second tragedy happened in a freak campus fraternity hazing incident. On February 2, 2017 Timothy Piazza, a 19-year-old sophomore engineering major who was pledging to join the Alpha Upsilon chapter of the Beta Theta Pi fraternity, was found severely injured in the basement of the fraternity house near campus after falling down a flight of 15 stairs. It was reported that Piazza had been subjected to an alcohol-fueled hazing fraternity ritual known as "The Gauntlet." He died the next day after lying helpless in the basement for nearly 12 hours before anyone decided to call 9-1-1 for medical assistance. One of the fraternity members, Ryan Burke, has plead guilty to nine charges. The fraternity's sophisticated security system revealed incriminating video footage of Timothy Piazza's nightmare that evening and the following morning.

While the Piazza death incident and trial is still unfolding, six Beta Theta Pi fraternity members have been arraigned on various charges, including involuntary manslaughter and aggravated assault following a months-long investigation into Piazza's death. Piazza's parents also filed a federal lawsuit against 28 members of the shuttered fraternity and St. Moritz Security Services, the security company that was hired by the fraternity to help enforce alcohol regulations at such events. The Piazza family reached a monetary settlement with Penn State University and Beta Theta Pi fraternity's national organization over their 19-year-old son's death.

Jim Piazza, the victim's father said, "I've said it before: This didn't have to happen. This is the result of a feeling of entitlement, flagrant disobedience of the law, and disregard for moral values that was then exacerbated by egregious acts of self-preservation. Again, this did not have to happen."

From a Culture standpoint, we agree with Mr. Piazza's statement. Everyone who has ever attended a college fraternity party knows there's the likelihood of free-flowing alcohol and other extracurricular activities that test the limits of the law. But in the case of Timothy Piazza, not only did every fraternity member involved in this tragedy fail to use common sense – just like the Penn State leadership in the Sandusky sex abuse scandal – they also ignored the values and principles embedded in their fraternity's Mission statement, which states: *To develop men of principle for a principled life.* The fraternity's Vision statement reads, *Every member will live Beta Theta Pi's values. Those values are: To build lasting bonds of friendship and brotherhood, Beta Theta Pi calls for Mutual Assistance, Intellectual Growth, Trust, Responsible Conduct, and Integrity.* Needless to say, the members of the Alpha Upsilon chapter of the Beta Theta Pi fraternity failed miserably on all counts, and now six members face criminal charges for their stupidity and irresponsible actions. In the end, not only is the brand of the fraternity severely tarnished, but it is one more dagger in the heart of Penn State University.

So the question must be asked, "Are these incidents just bad karma or random acts of misfortune that befell Penn State University? Or is there a deeper problem at PSU, one that is rooted in a Culture of corrupt leadership and poor decision-making skills that lead to such tragic incidents as the Sandusky sex abuse scandal and Timothy Piazza's death?

We know from our experience that such incidents don't just happen without the blessing or neglect of senior leadership. So this explains why inept and unconscious leaders will always bear the brunt of public criticism and negative fallout from shareholders, trustees and customers when bad things happen on their watch. As they should. In the case of PSU, such tragedies will continue to happen until the Board of Trustees and PSU leadership changes its Culture.

While Walter Reed Medical Center, the Veterans Administration, BP Oil, Wells Fargo, Penn State University and the Takata cases represent the extreme end of the spectrum, they each tell a gloomy story about how a company's leadership failed to promote and uphold core principles and values that were sacred to its founders. These revelations also accurately forecast what will happen to other companies, universities and government agencies that stray from doing the right things, and discourage employees from coming forward to blow the whistle when misguided managers attempt to take shortcuts or place profits ahead of customer safety, product reliability, environmental concerns and other priorities that are important to consumers.

In the case of United Airlines, an operations-driven mindset and dysfunctional Culture played a major part in the airlines' embarrassing incident on April 9, 2017. Dr. David Dao, a 69-year-old physician who was traveling on a paid ticket aboard United flight 3411 and was already seated on the departing airplane, was physically removed by Chicago airport police after he refused to surrender his seat to make room for several United employees who were trying to fly from Chicago to Louisville, Kentucky. The fiasco rocked the airline industry and resulted in a public relations firestorm for United Airlines when video went viral of Dr. Dao being beaten and dragged off the airplane. Dr. Dao sued United Airlines over his injuries and reached a settlement soon thereafter.

The dramatic incident forced major policy changes at United and other legacy airlines. Among those policy changes were the following:

1. Limit use of law enforcement to safety and security issues only.
2. Not require customers seated on the plane to give-up their seat involuntarily unless safety or security is at risk.
3. Increase customer compensation incentives for voluntary denied boarding up to $10,000.
4. Establish a customer solutions team to provide agents with creative solutions such as using nearby airports, other airlines or ground transportation to get customers to their final destination.
5. Ensure crews are booked onto a flight at least 60 minutes prior to departure.
6. Provide employees with additional annual training.
7. Create an automated system for soliciting volunteers to change travel plans.
8. Reduce the amount of overbooking.
9. Empower employees to resolve customer service issues in the moment.
10. Eliminate the red tape on permanently lost bags by adopting a "no questions asked" policy on lost luggage.

To United Airlines' credit, its CEO, Oscar Munoz, issued several apologies soon after the incident occurred and said he was going to do the right thing. Munoz said, "Every customer deserves to be treated with the highest level of service and the deepest sense of dignity and respect. Two weeks ago, we failed to meet that standard and we profoundly apologize. However, actions speak louder than words. Today we are taking concrete, meaningful action to make things right and ensure nothing like this ever happens again."

Dr. Dao's lawyer said, "United has taken full responsibility for what happened on Flight 3411 without attempting to blame others, including the city of Chicago. For this acceptance of corporate accountability, United is to be applauded."

The apology by United's Oscar Munoz was not only the right thing to do, but it minimized the damage to United Airlines' brand and reputation. Instead of keeping the story on the front page of newspapers, featured on the nightly television news, and allowing social media to blast United for its lack of sensitivity to passengers, Munoz recognized that United Airlines needed to fix its broken policies and procedures if it wanted to survive the Dr. Dao fiasco. So, by taking the steps he did to apologize for the mishandling of Dr. Dao, settling the lawsuit, and issuing ten fixes to United Airlines' broken policies relating to overbooking, Mr. Munoz nipped the negative press and probably saved his own job. Now Mr. Munoz is in the process of reshaping United Airlines' once-proud Culture so that United Airlines can restore its reputation and create an environment of service excellence. While it will be a long, hard road, we admire the fact that United Airlines' leadership has taken the first step – recognizing it must become a conscious business.

While every company and organization has shortcomings and, from time to time may falter in terms of living-up to its purpose and principles, there is a point when senior executives must step-in and grab the reins of leadership to get the organization back on track. Oscar Munoz demonstrated both humility and leadership in handling the fiasco that occurred aboard United Airlines Flight 3411.

But Mr. Munoz will undoubtedly need to do more. Specifically, United Airlines needs to go behind the scenes and examine how this incident occurred in the first place. What decisions were made and by whom? This should not be a witch hunt, but rather, it's important to find out exactly who took what steps and how those actions ultimately resulted in Dr. Dao's physical removal from his airplane seat. Only after this situation is fully analyzed will UAL be able to implement the necessary procedural changes and train its airport personnel not to repeat the same costly mistake.

Interestingly, we were flying through Chicago two days after the Dr. Dao story broke. An airline employee from another legacy airline who was working at the ticket counter remarked to us, "How stupid could UAL be? For $2,000 or less they could have bought Dr. Dao's seat and everyone would have been happy."

As we walked away from the ticket counter, Barbara and I remarked to each other, "No kidding! But nobody thought of doing that because it probably wasn't in their policies and procedures manual, and nobody at UAL was authorized to think outside the box!" This is unlike the Ritz-Carlton Hotels, which are renowned for outstanding customer service and where employees have the authority to do whatever is necessary to ensure their guests are satisfied. Regrettably, most companies do not empower their frontline employees to make decisions that will "save the day" for their customers. To the best of our knowledge, there have not been any cases reported of a Ritz-Carlton Hotel employee abusing this authority or squandering the hotel chain's money.

In each of these cases, it reinforces the fact that good people and good companies will sometimes do stupid things. Part of the problem stems from the fact that nobody in senior management has empowered the frontline to take actionable steps to protect the company's reputation and brand. Instead, employees are told to protect the bottom line at all costs! While the settlement terms of Dr. Dao's lawsuit have not been revealed, we will bet you dollars to donuts that it cost United Airlines much more than $10,000 or even $25,000 to settle his case. When you consider the public relations damage and the negative impact to UAL's bottom line, giving Dr. Dao $25,000 to give up his seat now makes perfect sense! Unfortunately, no one at UAL was thinking at that enlightened level on April 9, 2017.

Failure to empower your employees to take action and make smart decisions will only result in more problems for your organization, not to mention the possibility of costly litigation, negative publicity and, ultimately, the dismissal of your senior leadership.

Such is the price unconscious companies and organizations pay when their leaders' thoughts and actions are corrupted by greed, self-indulgence, neglect, bad decision-making, arrogance and plain old stupidity.

Conscious Business Take-Aways:

1. How do you define and shape your Culture so that it complements your brand and strengthens your bottom line?
2. Are your products and services good for the environment and the planet? How will Millennials know this to be the case? How do you get out the message that you care about your people and the planet?
3. Within your organization, are the truth tellers (aka whistleblowers) celebrated or punished and scorned? If a senior executive was about to make a bad decision, would anyone have the courage to keep him/her from making that decision? How do you know?

Chapter 2
What is Culture?

The Triad of Business Success™

Oftentimes we're asked by executives which aspects of Culture are the most important. In response to that question, we like to emphasize three legs of Culture because each of them is connected to the success of your brand. These three legs also inspire and motivate your people. They drive your performance and, ultimately, they impact your profitability. We refer to these three legs as your *Triad of Business Success™*. They are your Business Operations, Profit Strategies and Customer Relations. Each leg of this *Triad of Business Success™* links to The Five Ps, which we explain in greater detail in chapters 4-9. Let's examine each leg of the *Triad of Business Success™*.

Your Business Operations are the various functions and standard operations you perform on a daily basis to manage your business, maintain your workforce and serve your customers or clients. This leg of the *Triad of Business Success™* includes most of your major departments, including human resources, public relations, communications/social media, legal, risk management, accounting, payroll, budgeting, finance, compliance, IT, production, purchasing, facilities management and product services, to name but a few.

Conspicuous by their absence from Business Operations are several departments or functions – most noticeably are sales and product marketing, advertising/media, and your research and development departments. Interestingly, we classify these functions under the second leg, Profit Strategies, because they have a direct (instead of indirect) impact on your profitability and future brands.

We subscribe to the late management guru, Dr. Peter Drucker's thinking, who believed that profit is derived from the marketing and sales of your products and services. It was Dr. Drucker, along with IBM's Thomas Watson and former Parade magazine publisher, Arthur "Red" Motley, who are credited with the old axiom, "Nothing happens until somebody sells something!" They were all correct! These trailblazers were the real architects of Brand Management and how to position your products in the marketplace.

Dr. Drucker also believed that research and development, along with innovative thinking, were part of a company's profit strategy. This is why these departments belong as part of the Profit Strategies leg of the *Triad of Business Success*™.

The third leg of the *Triad of Business Success*™ is Customer Relations. Under this leg we find customer service, call centers, product and service warranties, and those research functions relating to customer data management and information technology. Again, paying tribute to Dr. Peter Drucker, we agree with his thesis that "the goal of every business is the acquisition and maintenance of its customers." Too often we have found that companies and government agencies fall short in their mission because they stop focusing on the "acquisition and maintenance" of their customers – both current and future customers.

What about the role of your employees when it comes to Customer Relations? We think Bill Marriott, Jr. of Marriott Hotels said it best when he wrote, "If we take care of our employees, they will take care of our customers/guests." And so, initiatives like Employee Engagement, Life Balance, and the spiritual wellbeing and development of your workplace are all closely linked to Customer Relations because committed employees will often make the difference between ensuring a customer's loyalty to the company or losing that customer for life.

In March 2017, the Forbes Human Resource Council published an article entitled, Five Important Training Topics You Don't Want to Overlook. We think this article is an excellent guide for every company that is serious about training its people. Here are the five topics the council recommended:

1. Embrace Shifts in Company Culture.

When putting together employee training, most companies overlook culture-based learning. It doesn't matter if this is a new hire or a 20-year veteran employee. Ongoing education around your culture and expectations is huge. Culture shifts as companies go through growth or organizational changes, and being in front of these changes to model desired behavior goes a long way.
- Lisa Whealon, GL Group, Inc.

2. Align Personal and Organizational Branding.

It's important that employees understand that their uniqueness is key to organizational success. However, it's also important that employees understand their personal branding must align with organizational branding and values. An employee's career success is not just about their performance, it's also about showing that they can perform in a manner that aligns with core organizational values.
- Bridgette Wilder, Media Fusion

3. Make Training More Accessible Through Mobile.

If training isn't accessible to everyone, it's no good. How can you duplicate the same training experience to remote employees or those who start after a training session is completed? Making training materials and media accessible via mobile devices allows all employees to be informed, increases your repeatability and scalability, and reduces headaches later on.

- Todd Richardson, Emplify

4. Expand Long-Term Skills.

Training should be connected to future employability, as well as the immediate position. This means an equal focus on helping them develop the skills they need now, and refining and expanding their skillset over time for future opportunities. It's motivating for employees to know their employer is invested in their growth and that what they're learning will be valuable to their career as a whole.

- Rick Devine, TalentSky, Inc.

5. Learn to Lead.

One often overlooked topic that employee training fails to address is how to be a leader rather than a manager. The word "manager" is a title; the label of "leader" should be for everyone. By teaching everyone in your company – top to bottom – to lead effectively, you will develop and grow existing talent, increase engagement, and become an employer of choice.

- Sarah O'Neill, Digital Trends

It's gratifying to see that first on the Forbes list is "Embrace Shifts in Company Culture." Lisa Whealon of the St. Louis-based GL group, Inc. is spot-on when she notes that most companies overlook Culture-based learning. Whealon's recommendation that companies provide ongoing training to new employees as well as 20-year veteran employees is a good idea because your Culture does shift, and all employees should be apprised of how Culture shifts affect them and their work. Training is a proven method for helping direct employee behavior to create positive customer outcomes.

Here's another well-known example that drives home the point of Culture training and the role Culture plays in the relationship between employees, customers and profits. It's a story from the annals of Stew Leonard's grocery stores, a family-owned and operated business based in Norwalk, Connecticut. The small chain of five grocery stores employs over 2,200 people and generates annual revenues of over $340 million. I first learned of this small but highly successful grocery store chain from Tom Peters, the author of *In Search of Excellence*. Stew Leonard's operates by two guiding principles that are embedded in its Culture.

The first of those two core principles are: Rule #1. The Customer is always right. Rule #2. If the Customer is ever wrong, reread Rule #1. This principle is so essential to the foundation of the Stew Leonard company that it is etched in a three-ton granite rock at each store's entrance.

The second core principle is this: "You can't have a great place to shop without first making it a great place to work." We agree. When a company has trouble keeping its best-and-brightest employees, something is wrong. We have found it can be traced to one of three root causes: low compensation -- management that does not grow or train its people, which causes key employees to leave -- or a volatile or toxic Culture.

Jill Leonard Tavello, who serves as the Executive Vice President of Culture and Communications at Stew Leonard's, is proud of her roots. She began working at the family store when she was just eight years old and barely tall enough to reach the cash

57

register. Jill believes the long-term success of her family-owned business and their legion of loyal shoppers is largely due to Stew Leonard's passionate approach to customer relations.

Twenty-five years ago, we had the pleasure of hearing Stew Leonard, Sr. speak about his service excellence strategy. During his speech, he shared a story about how he had lost a long-term customer and the painful lesson he learned from it. One day Mrs. Smith, who was a weekly shopper at Stew Leonard's, returned a melon she claimed to have bought from his store. She complained the melon was overripe and wanted a refund. Stew examined the melon and told her she couldn't have possibly bought the melon from his store because he didn't sell that type of melon. The amount in question was less than $2.00.

Furious that Stew challenged her, Mrs. Smith dropped the melon and exclaimed, "I'll never shop here again" and stormed out of the store. When Stew shared the incident with his wife later that evening, his wife asked, "How could you lose a $50,000 customer over a lousy melon? You should have given Mrs. Smith the two bucks!"

"You see," Stew explained to his audience, "My wife had it figured out. Mrs. Smith came into our store every week and spent about $100. That's $5,000 a year, and when you consider the lifelong value of a customer, well, in the case of Mrs. Smith that's at least ten years or $50,000. But I never thought of Mrs. Smith in those terms before. But I do now, and I'll never make that mistake again!"

In Search of Excellence author Tom Peters says Stew Leonard's figures were too low. Peters says there's a residual factor that Stew Leonard didn't consider. According to him, if Mrs. Smith was a typical consumer, she probably told five or more people about her negative encounter at Stew Leonard's store, and each of those five people probably told two or three others! So according to Tom

Peters, the ultimate impact to Stew Leonard's store as a result of mishandling Mrs. Smith and creating a negative customer experience was closer to $250,000 because at least four or five of her friends might stop shopping there as well. Now that's an expensive melon!

We first heard that story 25 years ago, and every time I see an employee, supervisor or manager arguing with a customer about something trivial – even when the customer is clearly wrong – it makes me wonder how many times the business "wins the battle" but loses the customer. Who amongst us hasn't had one of those "I'm never shopping here again" moments? The truth is, we rarely ever go back to that store or website because nobody likes to be hassled over a purchase when we have so many other options.

The sad part about all these "lost customer" moments is this – most companies never know why they lose customers like Mrs. Smith. Rarely will a disgruntled customer tell you the truth as to why they stopped doing business with your company after the fact. After 30 years of beating the "customer service" drum, it's surprising to hear about a company failing to ask their customers, *How are we doing?* and *How can we improve things around here for you?* or *What suggestions do you have to make your experience better with us?* These are basic questions, but to our amazement, most businesses fail to ask them.

Here's another important training question for your employees: *Does every employee in your organization understand the value and worth of a customer?* While some customers are worth more than others, our point is that every customer is worth something in terms of their spending power, referrals and social media comments. As we've previously stated and now emphasize strenuously, every customer has access to social media, and they can use it to blast your sterling reputation with negative reviews or they can sing your praises. What we like to know is this: are you creating Broadcast Customers or disgruntled customers? And how do you know?

We're not suggesting that it's fair or even a level playing field, but it is a fact that companies that mistreat customers or poorly handle customer grievances will likely lose those customers. Is it worth it to lose your customers? Consider the ultimate value and social media damage a disgruntled customer can cost your business. Maybe then, like Stew Leonard says, you'll give them the two bucks to save the relationship! Thinking about the value of each and every customer should be at the heart of your Culture.

Getting your corporate structure right and placing key departments under the correct leg in your *Triad of Business Success*™ is paramount to how you communicate each person's roles and responsibilities in your company. Some people might argue that the XYZ department belongs under a different leg, but we remain convinced that while certain departments have cross-over functions, where we have placed them is where they belong.

It should also be emphasized that each leg of the *Triad of Business Success*™ is dependent upon the other two. Like any triangle, it takes all three legs to stand firm and support the other two. So, when it comes to which department is most important, let's set the record straight. There can be no "Me First" justification because no single department is more important than any other. Every department should be recognized for their contribution to the growth and success of your company.

Consider this example that we hear frequently. The sales department might boast that they are the most important because they generate sales and new customers. And yes, while sales are strategic, without customer service support, a strong accounting function, or the weekly payroll being issued correctly, your sales department cannot properly function. Frankly, a salesperson is doomed without these vital supporting departments, let alone quality products or superior service.

The same case can be made for human resources, accounting, facilities management, legal and supplier management. Each department contributes to the success and profitability of your organization. Otherwise, why would management incur the expense of operating a costly department that doesn't help the bottom line?

When it comes to your profit strategies, as you look at your performance history and earnings over the past three years, it's important to recognize that Culture plays a significant role in both your top line (performance) and your bottom line (profitability). With very few exceptions, every company that has developed its Culture and leveraged it in the marketplace has improved its business operations, customer relations and delivered consistently strong profits.

Recently, three professors – Paul Gompers of Harvard, Andrew Metrick of Yale and Joy Ishii of Stanford – completed a comprehensive study on Corporate Culture. The result of their work has become known as the GMI Ratings. Not surprisingly, the professors found that one good proxy for Corporate Culture is a company's governance. In 2014, MSCI Inc. acquired GMI Ratings because of its popular focus on ESG (Environmental, Social and Governance) ratings and research to institutional investors. Its subsidiary, MSCI ESG Research Inc., now oversees the GMI Ratings process.

Market Watch, the popular online site owned by Dow Jones & Company, reported in 2014 on GMI Ratings' findings as it related to Corporate Culture. In addition to corporate governance factors, the risk management firm found that another good proxy for a company's internal Culture is the reliability and accuracy of a company's financial reporting. GMI concluded from its study that on average, the stocks with the best AGR (Accounting and Governance Risk) ratings have outperformed those with the worst.

We were intrigued to learn that GMI forensically analyzes the financial reporting and governance practices of over 8,500 North American-based publicly traded companies. In fact, companies that have a "Very Aggressive" AGR Score have a higher risk probability of facing negative events when compared to "Conservative" rated companies. Companies rated "Very Aggressive" under AGR have historically been:

- 10x more likely to face SEC enforcement actions.
- 6x more likely to delay financial reporting.
- 5X more likely to face securities litigation.
- 4X more likely to file for bankruptcy.
- 2X more likely to deal with executive officer change.

According to GMI's AGR ratings, the following eight firms ranked highest among the large-cap stocks in 2012:

Company	Current AGR Score (as of 3/13/12)	Average AGR Score (last four quarters	Market Value ($M)
		Large-Cap	
Avago Technologies	92	87	9,174
Boardwalk Pipeline Partners LP	92	89	5,737
Cincinnati Financial	97	98	5,824
Enbridge Energy Partners LP	96	77	7,236
Essex Property Trust	91	89	5,178
Progressive	91	94	13,845
Valhi	94	91	6,142
Whole Foods Market	79	74	15,678

In researching these eight companies' current market values, we found the following results through 2017: Avago Technologies' current market value is $40 billion; Boardwalk Pipeline Partnerships LP's current market value is $3.19 billion; Cincinnati Financial's current market value is $12.41 billion; Enbridge Energy Partners LP's current market value is $5.07 billion; Essex Property Trust's current market value is $16.27 billion; Progressive Corporation's current market value is $39.63 billion; Valhi, Inc.'s current market value is $1.15 billion; and Whole Foods Market's market value, before it was purchased by Amazon, was listed in August 2018 as $11.6 billion. Without exception, all eight of the top-ranked companies in GMI's study performed exceptionally well.

Forbes magazine recently published its 2017 list of The 100 Most Trustworthy Companies in America using the GMI criteria that include: high risk behaviors like regulatory actions, amended filings, revenue and expense recognition methods, and bankruptcy risk. Companies are scored on a 1 to 100-point scale, with 70 being the lowest score to appear on this year's list. The list is divided into three categories: Large Cap, Mid Cap, and Small Cap. Many companies on the list are not household names.

For example, the top five companies in the Large Cap category are: CR Bard Inc.; CenterPoint Energy, Inc.; Edwards Lifesciences Corp; Host Hotels & Resorts Inc.; and Hubbell Incorporated.

In the Mid Cap category, the top five companies are: AAON, Inc.; Apogee Enterprises, Inc.; Badger Meter, Inc.; Big Lots, Inc.; and Boise Cascade Company.

In the Small Cap category, the top five companies are: Alamo Group, Inc.; Alpha and Omega Semiconductor Ltd.; American Public Education, Inc.; Bazaarvoice, Inc.; and Big 5 Sporting Goods Company.

While a company's stock performance is but one factor in the overall calculation of the importance of a company's Culture, it is a significant factor because every CEO's job depends on their stockholders' satisfaction with earnings. It's the key metric by which every CEO keeps their job or is terminated. While we believe that a company's quarterly earnings may be overrated in terms of its long-term importance to the success of a business, ironically, this is the one metric that leadership has chosen to be judged by. This is why so many CEOs live or die by their quarterly numbers. Shareholders and market analysts want financial results, and how a company's Culture impacts sales and customer relationships is directly tied to its financial performance. This is one more key reason why senior leadership should focus on their Culture. It directly impacts the bottom line.

Lou Gerstner, the former chairman and CEO of RJR Nabisco and IBM, who is credited with reviving the ailing tech giant in the 1990s and now serves as chairman of the board at the Broad Institute of MIT and Harvard, described Culture this way:

"What is critical to understand here is that people do not do what you expect but what you inspect. Culture is not a prime mover. Rather it is a derivative. It forms as a result of signals employees get from the corporate processes that structure their work priorities.

"Compensation is one of the most important of these processes. If the reward system pays a premium for one kind of behavior, that's what will determine employee behavior – regardless of the words enshrined in the value statement.

"If the financial-reporting system focuses entirely on short-term operating results, that's what will get priority from employees. If you want employees to care a lot about customers, then customer-satisfaction data should get as prominent a place in the reporting system as sales and profit.

"Look at who gets the atta-boy and atta-girl treatment at corporate meetings. Is it the leaders in meeting financial targets – or is it those who raise concerns regarding marketing programs that give priority to corporate goals at the expense of true customer needs?

"And those sincere expressions of commitment to diversity by the CEO? Obviously helpful. But what really matters is which programs suggested by the HR department – such as executive coaches, neutral-gender parental leave and others – actually get through the budgeting process. Believe me, the budget process is almost as powerful as the compensation process in shaping corporate Culture.

"It is the cumulative effect of all of these processes: compensation, performance measurement, recognition, etc. that shape what we describe as corporate Culture.

"So for any CEO who wants to understand the real Culture in his or her company: Do not look at the value statement in the new employee handbook. Go deep and understand what each process in the company is telling employees is important. Again, people do not do what you expect, but what you inspect."

We couldn't agree more with Mr. Gerstner's comments and we address the importance of work processes in Chapter 8 of this book. What we find interesting about Lou Gerstner's comments on Culture at IBM is the "me first" attitude and a lack of clarity of direction from the top down.

When he arrived at IBM to assume the role of CEO, as he notes in the article below, he found a lack of teamwork and too many employees not focused on solving the customers' problems. Gerstner admits he learned two very valuable lessons. First, "Culture is everything," and second, "customers want solutions."

In 2002, Martha Lagace of HBS Working Knowledge wrote about Lou Gerstner's lecture to a Harvard Business School MBA class. Specifically, Mr. Gerstner talked about Culture and the important role Culture played in the growth and transformation of IBM during his tenure as CEO.

Here's an excerpt from Martha Lagace's article:

"These days, Gerstner sees the basis of IBM's subsequent transformation as wholly cultural. When he joined, however, it was not at all clear where the problem lay. In his first three months on the job, he didn't spend "an hour" thinking about culture, although he learned a lot about it without trying. There was the IBM culture of crisp white shirts, the culture of hordes of administrative assistants, and the culture, most debilitating, of the individual with a capital "I," of me-first for every employee."

"IBM's extraordinary success in the '60s and '70s was built on one of the most dynamic sales cultures in the world," he said. In his various roles before joining IBM, he was often a customer for the famously dynamic IBM salespeople. "They were very good, very relentless, very focused. And very individualistic."

That kind of individualism and decentralization had served Big Blue well for many years, but by the 1980s and early 1990s it was no longer tenable. He saw that the company needed to come together to survive.

"We needed to integrate as a team inside the company so that we could integrate for the customers on their premises. It flew in the face of what everybody did in their careers before I arrived there. It meant that we would share technical plans, we would move toward common technical standards and plans, we would not have individual transfer pricing between every product so that everybody could get their little piece of the customers' money," he said.

"Very few companies in the world today can afford to indulge in unique systems for every office branch," he said.

"Most managers in corporate life these days fixate on strategy as their way of envisioning company transformation," Gerstner said. Strategy work by itself, though "terribly important," is not enough to save a dying company. "You don't 'win' with strategy," he said. "Everybody's strategy in industry is fairly similar. There's no way to create a unique strategy. You can have a good one, but you can expect that your competitors are going to emulate it every day."

Under Gerstner, IBM's new strategy was to use processes and culture to regain advantage. Moving from proprietary standards to open standards, for example, was important to IBM's new strategy, and the ramifications for processes and culture were enormous. Using IBM's technological finesse to make solutions for customers in addition to just creating fancy technology was also a key to its new strategy. Customers wanted solutions, he'd said. They didn't want to know what their equipment ran on.

"In our case we were able to define a strategic path that made sense," he said, adding that the strategic path was not altogether different from what some people at IBM had been espousing before he arrived. But now, a united culture gave IBM's strategy the speed and effectiveness that was missing before. The Internet was certainly a galvanizing force, too. The company had spent $800 million per year for the last nine years on process transformation, he'd said, and it is now transforming the process systems once again to make them all network-enabled.

Underneath all the sophisticated processes, Gerstner concluded, there is always the company's sense of values and identity.

"It took me to age fifty-five to figure that out. I always viewed culture as one of those things you talked about, like marketing and advertising. It was one of the tools that a manager had at his or her disposal when you think about an enterprise."

He added, "The thing I have learned at IBM is that culture is everything."

Source: Martha Lagace, Harvard Business Review Working Knowledge, December 9, 2002. Gerstner: Changing Culture at IBM - Lou Gerstner Discusses Changing the Culture at IBM.

Conscious Business Take-Aways:

1. How do you define Culture? Do your senior executives understand that Culture is the energetic presence of your company as seen through the eyes of your employees, customers and suppliers? That presence is felt by everyone who comes into contact with your company.

2. What is your average customer worth to your business? Do your employees know and understand the true value of a customer? It's a key component of acquiring and maintaining your customers.

3. Does your senior leadership see Culture as a competitive advantage or do they treat it as a burden that restricts their ability to manage?

Chapter 3

The Culture Spectrum™:
Every Company Has a Culture. What's Yours?

Because there are so many different types of companies and organizations, and each one has its own unique Culture, we don't believe you can simply place Company X in a box and state emphatically that because Google and Disney thrive on innovation, theirs is a Culture of innovation or, because Berkshire Hathaway focuses on the art of the deal and generating a high return on its investments, theirs is a Culture of revenue growth. Frankly, Culture is much more complicated than that.

Having studied over 830 companies, organizations and government agencies during the past six years, we designed a *Culture Spectrum*™ comprised of four quadrants that each and every entity we studied fits into comfortably. Here they are:

High Performance Culture	Balanced Culture
Under-Performing Culture	Volatile Culture

Before we examine the features of each quadrant, let's explain a few key points about the *Culture Spectrum*™.

First, companies and organizations are evolving entities. When they stop evolving, they atrophy and die. Did you know that of the Fortune 500 list of top companies in 1955, only 60 remain on the list? That's a mere 12 percent. The world is ever-changing, and the wants and needs of consumers have not only dramatically changed the *face* of business, but also the way companies do business.

It was Fred Tuffile, a professor at Bentley University in Waltham, Massachusetts who said, "The biggest advantage that new start-up companies have over established businesses is a blank piece of paper." In other words, they start fresh. They have no baggage, just big dreams, unlimited possibilities and very limited experience with failure. They don't know the meaning of "no." They don't understand boundaries because they have never set boundaries. Basically, every one of the wonder-companies launched since the 1980s has been founded by people who were risk-takers. They had everything to win and nothing to lose. They went "all-in" as the expression goes, and for many, their gambles paid off in the billions!

This explains in part the rapid rise of start-up wonders like Apple, Google, Microsoft, Amazon, Tencent, Yahoo!, Baidu, eBay, Alibaba Group and Facebook. But it also explains how long-established brands like Coca-Cola, Johnson & Johnson, Disney, 3M, Abbott Labs, Avon Products, Ashland, Boeing, Hershey, General Motors, Ford and United Technologies got their start many decades ago and adhered to proven cultural values and principles which have served them well for over 60 years. The fact is, many of these successful companies started in a similar fashion; some in a garage and others as the brainchild of a handful of people who had a brilliant idea and knew how to build a better mousetrap. As Napoleon Hill, the author of *Think and Grow Rich*, suggested, "Every great achievement known to man started as someone's idea." So once the idea takes root, but before the product is launched, something happens within the organization that defines it. This is the undercurrent of Culture. Oftentimes, the cultural fabric of an organization is an extension of its founders. It's a reflection of their passion, zeal, creativity, innovation, never-say-die attitude, and untiring devotion to their idea. Walt Disney, Herb Kelleher of Southwest Airlines, and Apple's Steve Jobs were such persons. Initially, these entrepreneurial dreamers began by hiring people who believed in their (the founder's) dream. Then this small, dedicated core of people built, shaped and molded the Culture of the organization through their innovative spirit, hard work, sweat, and throwing ideas against the wall to see which would stick. This is the origin and Culture evolution of every organization.

Over the years, a company's Culture is shaped as the organization evolves and leadership changes. But as we discovered in our research, in most cases if you turn back the pages far enough to the early days of a company, you will discover that the heart and soul of its Culture is rooted in the founder's dream and vision. Interestingly, the same is true of a nation. We need only look at the Founding Fathers of the United States of America to appreciate this fact. Without exception, we know that the cultural fabric of a company, organization and nation sprang from the heart and soul of its leaders. Why? Because it's the leaders who set the theme, vision and goals of the organization. Yes, shareholders and employees have some say, but ultimately it's the CEO, President or Chairman who sets the organization's direction and, therefore, refines its Culture. This is why we believe the CEO is also the de facto Chief Culture Officer. The buck stops at the top.

When an organization is blessed with remarkable leadership – as was the case with GM's Alfred Sloan or England's Winston Churchill, the organization rises to the occasion and performs at its peak. Unfortunately, the opposite happens when a leader is weak, uninspiring and lacks vision. The corporate graveyard is littered with hundreds of such examples, and so are the history books.

It was the Scottish writer Thomas Carlyle who, in the 1840s, introduced the "Great Man" theory. Carlyle held the belief that history – and the advancement of civilization – could largely be explained by a handful of highly influential individuals who, because of their great gifts (e.g., intellect, charisma, vision, communication skills and political adeptness), were able to fully realize their power in a way that had a decisive historical impact. Carlyle's "Great Man" theory also explains how leaders develop and manipulate an organization's Culture to create a cult-like devotion to the goals set forth by that particular leader. This explains how a handful of magnificent visionaries have shaped our world. Consider these luminaries and how they changed our world: Abraham Lincoln, Henry Ford, Mahatma Gandhi, Andrew Carnegie, Steve Jobs, Warren Buffet, Lee Iacocca, Bill Gates, Louis Pasteur, Elvis Presley, Charles Darwin, Julius Caesar, Hippocrates II, Galileo Galilei, Christopher Columbus, Isaac Newton, Michelangelo di Lodovico Buonarroti Simoni, Wolfgang Amadeus Mozart, Leonardo da Vinci, Jesus Christ, Alexander the Great and Aristotle, to name but a few.

What is it about a certain person like President John F. Kennedy or a group of people like The Beatles, who can capture the hearts and souls of millions of people – and even generations – and make them believers and followers? We think at its root it's cultural. This also explains how madmen like Adolf Hitler, Joseph Stalin, Mao Zedong, Pol Pot, Idi Amin, Osama bin Laden and Saddam Hussein could arouse the negative emotions of a nation and produce a Culture of fear and hatred that turned a discontent and restless society against each other and the world.

Culture is a very powerful tool. This is why it should only be entrusted to leaders who have a good heart and reflective soul.

When this happens, the results are good. When it doesn't happen, employees, society and nations will suffer.

As we developed the attributes of each quadrant on our *Culture Spectrum™*, we identified five factors that all companies and organizations can be measured by. We refer to these factors as the Five Ps. They are: Purpose, Principles, People, Processes and Performance. These factors are applicable to every business or organization, regardless of its product or service, size, location, leadership structure or industry. Each of the Five Ps are discussed in greater detail in Chapters 4-9.

In determining where your organization falls on the *Culture Spectrum™*, you can assess its position using the following four quadrants:

High-Performance Culture = 80 – 100%	Balanced Culture = 65 – 79%
Under-Performing Culture = 50 – 64%	Volatile <50%

The most desirable placement is in the upper left quadrant, a *High-Performance Culture*. A *High-Performance Culture* is defined as an organization that has each of the Five Ps in place and is doing an excellent job implementing the tenants of the Five Ps.

A *Balanced Culture* is defined as an organization that has each of the Five Ps in place and is doing a superior job implementing the tenants of the Five Ps.

An *Under Performing Culture* is defined as an organization that has some elements of each of the Five Ps in place but has trouble managing its people, processes and performance, and, therefore, the organization is doing a below-average job implementing the tenants of the Five Ps and achieving its desired results.

A *Volatile Culture* is defined as an organization that has some aspects of the Five Ps in place, but has serious challenges creating positive outcomes, results and profits because its Purpose, Principles and Processes are not aligned, its people are under-performing, and its Performance is lagging.

Using the Five Ps, we've defined what it takes for a company to rank in the top, upper-left quadrant:

1. A *High-Performance Culture* company has clarity of purpose. Every successful organization we studied is a purposeful entity. In other words, the mission, vision and goals of the organization are clearly articulated to employees, customers and suppliers. The organization's purpose is also specific to that entity. Its purpose explains how it will achieve its goals in specific terms, the void it will fill in the marketplace and, in doing so, attract customers; how it accounts for competitive positioning; the metrics used by the company to measure progress and outcomes; how it will educate and train its employees and suppliers to achieve excellent results; and finally, painting a realistic picture of the challenges and threats facing the organization.

A good example of a purposeful organization is Sharp Healthcare, a Malcolm Baldrige Award winner based in San Diego, California. Sharp has four acute-care hospitals, three specialty hospitals and two affiliated medical groups. In 2013, Becker's named it to its list of "100 Integrated Systems to Know." Sharp is known for outstanding healthcare that it brands as the "Sharp Experience." Sharp has a sterling reputation when it comes to patient engagement, training its professional and medical staff, advanced technology, and active communication from senior leadership to all employees. Michael Murphy, Sharp Healthcare's CEO from 1996-2019, was most proud of Sharp's All-Staff Assembly. Sharp recently had its 15th annual assembly, which brings the Sharp team together to celebrate, refresh and renew so it's able to be the best it can be for its patients and community. The recent All-Staff Assembly was attended by more than 14,000 people over the three-day event. Murphy said, "It has a huge impact on our organization and Culture. It's energizing to have been through it and to have celebrated the wonderful things the people of Sharp do."

Murphy was also proud of the relaunched Sharp.com website which has been updated and modernized during his tenure as CEO. In addition, he was proud of the Sharp News Room, which can be accessed through the Sharp.com website. Each day, Sharp posts two to four news stories about what's happening at Sharp and what's trending in healthcare. This keeps the staff informed and focused on Sharp's priorities.

We also like Costco, the discount wholesaler that had its roots in San Diego when Sol Price launched FedMart in the 1950s. Mr. Price then created another warehouse store called Price Club in 1976, which Costco eventually bought. Today, Costco has over 750 stores worldwide and interestingly, it's considered one of America's largest pizza chains because it sells so much pizza at its food courts! When Walmart founder Sam Walton was searching for a name for his new retail stores, he credits Sol Price with helping to create part of the Walmart name. He told Mr. Price that he had decided on the Walmart name after seeing the name FedMart on Sol Price's store during a visit to San Diego in the 1950s.

When Costco's 91 million members (yes, Costco sells memberships at a very reasonable cost) shop at Costco, they tend to buy in bulk. The average Costco shopper spent over $160 per visit in 2017. Another curious fact is that Costco spends no money on advertising. This means lower prices and more savings for its member-customers.

Its employees are properly trained, dedicated and well-paid. As of late 2017, Costco paid its hourly workers an average of nearly $21.00 per hour, not including overtime. This is nearly twice the $12.00 per hour minimum wage of California's hourly workers as of January 1, 2019.

By comparison, in April 2017, Walmart paid an average wage of $12.67 for full-time employees in the U.S. according to a letter it sent to activist Ralph Nader.

There is also some question as to the accuracy of this data since Walmart announced in October that it would boost its starting wage to $11.00 per hour. Target, another retail competitor, said it would raise its minimum wage to $15.00 per hour by 2020. Amazon, who many retail experts view as the ultimate competitor, has fueled the minimum wage battle by declaring it plans to pay all employees at least $15.00 per hour in 2019. Such major shifts in hourly compensation will force every major retailer to rethink their wages and benefits if they want to attract and maintain a capable, dedicated workforce.

88% of Costco employees also have company-sponsored health insurance. Walmart says that more than half of its employees have company-sponsored health insurance. Costco workers with health coverage pay premiums that amount to less than 10 percent of the overall cost of their plans. It treats its employees well in the belief that a happier work environment will result in a more profitable company. "I just think people need to make a living wage with health benefits," says Costco CEO Craig Jelinek. "It also puts more money back into the economy and creates a healthier country. It's really that simple."

2. A *High-Performance Culture* company operates as a Principle-based entity. An organization's principles should reflect its commitment to people, its marketplace, its communities and the environment. A *High-Performance Culture* is one where leaders not only preach and reinforce the organization's principles, but also adhere to them. A good example of a principle-based company is Swiss-based Nestlé, the world's largest food and beverage company, which was established in 1866. In a manifesto issued by its chairman, Nestlé articulated the following principles which it adheres to today. This document is available in more than 50 languages, and reflects the basic ideas of fairness, honesty and a concern for individuals and families, communities and the planet:

1. The nutrition, health and wellness of its consumers.
2. Quality assurance and product safety.
3. Consumer communication, human rights and fair labor practices.
4. Human rights in our business activities.
5. Leadership and personal responsibility.
6. Safety and health at work.
7. Supplier and customer relations.
8. Agriculture and rural development.
9. Environmental sustainability.
10. Water.

Another example of a company that has adopted and embraced core principles to guide it through the rapidly changing global marketplace is Mitsubishi Corporation. At Mitsubishi, three corporate principles are the foundation of the vision and strategy for its commitment to corporate social responsibility:

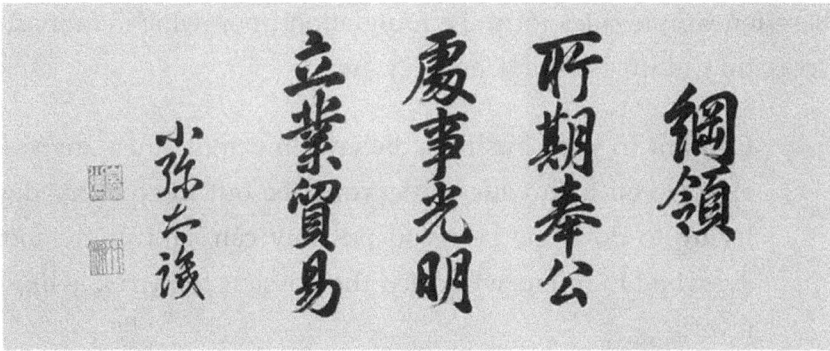

Corporate Responsibility to Society
"Shoki Hoko"

Strive to enrich society, both materially and spiritually, while contributing towards the preservation of the global environment.

Integrity and Fairness
"Shoji Komei"

Maintain principles of transparency and openness, conducting business with integrity and fairness.

Global Understanding Through Business
"Ritsugyo Boeki"

Expand business, based on an all-encompassing global perspective.

We also like Walmart, the Number One company among the Fortune 500 list. While Walmart has its share of critics, we think the company deserves credit for getting it right most of the time. After all, you don't get to the Number One ranking on the Fortune 500 list and stay there for six years in a row without doing most things right. Consider this fact; as of March 2018, Walmart had revenues of $500.3 billion, which was more than twice as much as the number two company on the Fortune 500 list, Exxon Mobil.

At the core of Walmart's success is its adherence to founder Sam Walton's guiding principles for running a successful business.

These ten simple rules form the foundation upon which Walmart's successful Culture is built. Here they are:

1. **Commit to your business.** Believe in it more than anybody else. If you love your work, you'll be out there every day, trying to do it the best you possibly can, and pretty soon everybody around will catch the passion from you – like a fever.

2. **Share your profits with all your associates, and treat them as partners.** In turn, they will treat you as a partner, and together you will all perform beyond your wildest expectations.

3. **Motivate your partners.** Money and ownership alone aren't enough. Set high goals, encourage competition, and then keep score. Don't become too predictable.

4. **Communicate everything you possibly can to your partners.** The more they know, the more they'll understand. The more they understand, the more they'll care. Once they care, there's no stopping them.

5. **Appreciate everything your associates do for the business.** Nothing else can quite substitute for a few well-chosen, well-timed, sincere words of praise. They're absolutely free – and worth a fortune.

6. **Celebrate your success.** Don't take yourself so seriously. Loosen up, and everybody around you will loosen up. Have fun. Show enthusiasm – always. All of this is more important, and more fun, than you think, and it really fools competition.

7. **Listen to everyone in your company.** And figure out ways to get them talking. To push responsibility down in your organization, and to force good ideas to bubble up within it, you must listen to what your associates are trying to tell you.

8. **Exceed your customers' expectations.** Give them what they want — and a little more. Make good on all your mistakes, and don't make excuses — apologize. Stand behind everything you do.

9. **Control your expenses better than your competition.** This is where you can always find the competitive advantage. You can make a lot of different mistakes and still recover if you run an efficient operation. Or you can be brilliant and still go out of business if you're too inefficient.

10. **Swim upstream.** Go the other way. Ignore the conventional wisdom. If everybody else is doing it one way, there's a good chance you can find your niche by going in exactly the opposite direction.

3. A *High-Performance Culture* company takes pride in its people and cares about them. An organization's commitment to its people is at the heart and soul of a High-Performance corporate Culture because people are largely responsible for the success and profitability of their organization. When we write about people, we are including employees, suppliers and customers. This is an important triangle of success that requires your organization to give equal emphasis to each leg of the triangle – employees, suppliers and customers. If one area is deficient, the triangle will eventually collapse.

A good example of a company that gets it right when it comes to demonstrating a *High-Performance Culture* with its people is Amadeus, the Madrid-based company established in 1988 by an alliance among Air France, Lufthansa, Iberia and SAS to develop a Global Distribution System (GDS), a worldwide computerized reservation network that would use a single point of access to connect airlines' content with travel agencies and consumers to provide real-time search, pricing, booking, ticketing and other processing solutions. Amadeus began operations in 1992 and has emerged as a global leader in its field. It prides itself on its purpose – to shape the future of travel. As Amadeus says, "Travel broadens horizons, creates connections and builds economies. Travel powers progress and Amadeus powers travel."

With over 17,000 employees worldwide, Amadeus always draws favorable ratings from its employees. On Indeed, an independent website that evaluates companies and their work environment, several employees at Amadeus praised their company for its flexible hours, home office environment, creativity, semi-frequent travel and the opportunity to advance. They noted that management was very approachable and understanding. They also noted that the most difficult part of the job was keeping current with industry changes.

When it comes to creating a Culture of excellence in the workplace and taking care of your people – including suppliers and customers – it's not enough to merely show appreciation in the form of quarterly pizza parties, birthday gift cards and year-end bonuses. If this is all you're doing, you're missing the mark. Most importantly, your employees want to be appreciated for who they are and the talents they bring to the job. They want to be nurtured and valued. They don't want to be harassed and they certainly don't want to be treated like children. This requires managers to be professional, respectful and positive mentors. It also requires managers to sharpen their listening skills and give constructive feedback – note the word constructive – that helps the employee to do a better job and utilize their Core Powers.

Finally, managers need to stand up for their employees, especially when senior management is wrong. Yes, it takes guts and courage, but this is the best way we know of for a manager to earn the respect and loyalty of his/her employees.

Suppliers and customers also need to be nurtured. The biggest complaint we hear from suppliers of major companies is a lack of communication and, quite often, miscommunication. It's important for your supply chain to get it right the first time. To do this, it requires clarity of direction, clear communication from the top down, and specific instructions to your valued suppliers on what they need to do to get the job done right the first time, on schedule and within budget.

With regards to your customers, the number one complaint they have with companies is limited access. In other words, they can't reach you! While Millennials are a growing market segment, many Baby Boomers (and other customers) still prefer that good old human touch. So it's important that your customers are able to easily reach you by telephone, email and via your website. When writing this book, we audited over 100 popular companies and found that fewer than 35 of those companies made it easy for customers to find their telephone number or locate a Customer Service point-of-contact. Furthermore, the company's address was buried in their website, if it was listed at all. Finally, 37 companies only offered an email response option for contacting the business. This is contrary to what most of your customers want and need in order to do business with you. Why not make it easy for your customers to communicate and connect with you?

Remember that while your webmasters and IT folks are very good at what they do, they may not be skilled in the art of customer relations so be sure your customer service, marketing and sales team review your website to ensure it is customer-friendly and easy to navigate – especially in terms of reaching your company by telephone, email, or locating a mailing address. We believe this information should be on at least your website's home page. The best website we've seen that is easy to navigate, user-friendly and offers non-punitive customer policies is Southwest Airlines (www.southwest.com). Check it out.

Here's the bottom line. The harder you make it for your customers to navigate your website or contact you, the more customers you will lose. The sad part is you'll never know why because they rarely tell you how difficult your website is to navigate.

4. A *High-Performance Culture* company has proven Processes that work. In the 1990s, many companies focused on their work processes – how they did what they do – in order to streamline their work flow and production lines. This effort led to Six Sigma and other progressive systemic improvements for making products faster, better and cheaper. It was Dr. W. Edwards Deming, the father of the Quality Revolution, who refocused Japanese and American companies on the importance of quality and excellence in the workplace. Deming emphasized that every product or service is produced through a process, and the easier the process, the easier it will be for your employees to produce it – faster, better and cheaper. The questions we encourage senior leadership to ask when it comes to your work processes are these:

1. Do you have the right people doing the job?
2. Have you adequately trained your people to do their job? Remember, everyone learns differently so individual training, coaching and mentoring are the keys to creating the best results.
3. Do your people have the tools, resources and systems in place that they need to get the job done right the first time?

4. Is management supportive of its people and the work to be done? Remember, your employees need a champion who will fight for them.

5. A *High-Performance Culture* company has proven Results to validate its Performance. While *The Heart and Soul of Culture* emphasizes the importance of "people before profits," we recognize and support an organization's initiative to create excellent outcomes. This includes making a profit. As we have stated many times, we believe that profitability can best be achieved and enhanced through your people. How do you help your people create a winning performance, which leads to generous profits?

Throughout this book, we've discussed the importance of engaging your employees by giving them meaningful work and the necessary tools and resources to accomplish positive results. Later in the book we discuss the importance of letting your employees write their own unique job description so they can leverage their talents and abilities in the workplace. It does not benefit your organization to limit an employee's use of their talents. We've emphasized the importance of training your employees and suppliers and designing your work processes in such a way that whatever you produce or provide is done in an efficient way. We've also discussed the connection between having a clear purpose and strong principles to keep your business on track and steer clear of troubled waters.

This is how you achieve a winning performance. Companies that land in the *High-Performance Culture* quadrant are doing these things right. Yes, they are doing them in various ways and achieving different levels of success, but they are doing them, and customers have taken notice and like doing business with these companies because they are aligned with the same values as their customers. This is how you create success. This is how you create a Culture of excellence in the workplace. Frankly, it's not rocket science, but it does require strong leadership, courage and an unwavering commitment to champion positive change. As Pat Riley, the legendary NBA basketball coach once said, "It may be simple, but it isn't easy!"

Conscious Business Take-Aways:

1. As you look at our *Culture Spectrum*™, where would you place your company? Are you High-Performance, Balanced, Volatile or Under-Performing? Ask your customers and employees because they know and they will tell you!

2. At your company's annual strategic planning meeting do you start with a blank piece of paper as suggested by Professor Fred Tuffile or do you simply add on to what's been done the previous year?

3. Have you upgraded your approach to human resources by allowing your employees to write their own job descriptions so you can use all their talents and abilities in the workplace? If not, when will you? If so, what changes have you seen in terms of improved productivity, retention and loyalty to the company?

Chapter 4
The Five Ps of Culture

For two decades we've studied corporate Culture, and during that time we've narrowed down the many attributes and qualities of corporate Culture to five key factors. As previously mentioned, we refer to them as "The Five Ps of Culture." They are: Purpose, Principles, People, Processes and Performance. When evaluating an organization's Culture, it's essential to identify those things that make it unique. A company's cultural attributes extend beyond its brand. Culture is more than simply a company's products and people. And, certainly, it's more than last quarter's financial performance.

We've determined that an organization's Culture can be measured if properly assessed. Frankly, the challenge for us in defining Culture as a measurable dimension of every organization was determining those key factors that are pillars of every organization's Culture and, at the same time, can be measured through a methodical assessment. In the final analysis, we found only five attributes that met our criteria. This is how we arrived at The Five Ps of Culture.

It's important to reiterate one of our central themes to this book – Culture matters. If you don't acknowledge and embrace what you stand for – that is, your Culture – how can you expect your employees, customers, suppliers and other stakeholders to hold your organization in high regard? Without exception, ignoring one or more of the Five Ps is at the root cause of every company or institution's fall from grace. It is the Five Ps of Culture that will provide you with a clear view of who you really are and how you are perceived in the real world that lies just beyond your front door. Let's explore each one of the Five Ps from the viewpoint of a Culture Assessment.

Purpose:

From a Culture perspective we want to know the following:
Does your organization have a clearly defined mission and purpose for being in business? Without a clearly defined purpose or mission, an organization will drift into eventual extinction.

Do your leaders support its mission and vision? This might strike you as a rather odd question, but we have witnessed many organizations, especially in the political and government realm, where leaders have been tasked with dismantling an agency or department because a governor, mayor or president doesn't want to fund its mission or purpose. We've also seen dozens of cases where venture capital vultures have bought a company to eliminate the competition or to dismantle most of the business for the sake of preserving one sacred cow – such as a popular brand or product.

We also want to know if an organization invests in its people by teaching them about its purpose, mission, vision and goals. It's shocking to see how many organizations do not properly orient new employees by explaining its history, purpose, mission, vision and goals. How do leaders expect a new employee, supplier or contractor to pledge their allegiance to the organization if they have no clue as to its proud history and purpose? People need to know how they fit into an organization and what role they play. Otherwise, people will be reluctant to get engaged and they'll lack commitment and initiative.

Finally, we want to know if the organization is respected as an industry leader. When performance suffers, oftentimes we can trace the cause to a lack of pride among its employees. Nobody wants to work for a loser, and everybody loves a winner. This is especially true among Millennials and Gen Z'ers who want to work for ethical organizations that benefit society and do good things for the community, the environment and the planet.

Principles:

In evaluating an organization's Culture, we want to know:

Does the organization have clearly defined principles and values that it adheres to? Does your organization know the difference between right and wrong? If so, does your organization do the right and honorable thing?

Does your organization value and respect its employees, customers and suppliers? If so, how?

Is your organization willing to admit mistakes? If so, who is blamed, if anybody?

How does your organization try to improve its image and credibility with customers, suppliers and other stakeholders? Does your company celebrate the success of its employees – not only on the job, but their personal achievements? Does your company share its best practices with others (including competitors) in your industry? Does your organization encourage employees to be involved in their local community and local charitable activities?

People:

In evaluating your organization's Culture, we want to know about your People and the organization's relationship to its employees, customers, suppliers and other key stakeholders. Here are some of the key questions we ask:

Does management listen to employees and invite feedback?

Does your company put the interest, safety and wellbeing of people above profits? Does your organization strive to hire the best possible talent within its budget or do you pinch pennies at the expense of attracting and keeping your best-and-brightest talent?

Is your management trained and skilled in asking questions and getting feedback from customers, employees, suppliers and other key stakeholders?

Are your employees dedicated to the organization to the point that they are willing to go the extra mile to finish important tasks and projects on time?

Is there an attitude of "above-and-beyond-the-call-of-duty" among your employees when it comes to customer service?

When a new employee is hired, does your organization have in place a process to ensure all new employees are formally welcomed, trained and integrated into the team? A new employee should never feel unwelcomed or neglected when they first start their new job.

Does your organization embrace diversity?

Does your organization have a zero-tolerance policy on harassment that applies to all genders?

Does your organization actually treat employees equally and fairly?

How does your organization address delicate issues like bias in the workplace and employee misconduct? Is every employee held to the same high standards and rules?

Processes:
In evaluating an organization's Culture, we want to know if it has clearly defined processes so work flows smoothly and everybody understands their role in creating a successful outcome. Some of the questions we ask that provides us insight to your processes are the following:

Are your employees open to new ideas and new ways of doing things? How do you know?

How often do you require your employees to review their workflow processes and request changes or improvements?

Are your suppliers trained and educated in ways that support the success of your business?

Do your suppliers adhere to the principles and standards set by your organization? How do you measure this?

Do your employees have the necessary knowledge and skills to do their work and improve their work processes?

What is your process for continuously improving your products and services, especially your leading brands?

How does your company provide the continued flow of vital information to ensure your people and operations can perform at peak levels?

Does your company value the use of data and information to ensure cybersecurity and strengthen customer relationships?

Does your organization encourage and financially support continuous learning for every employee?

Does your organization have emergency plans to safeguard its people, technology, infrastructure, data and information in the event of a disaster?

Performance:

Finally, from a Culture perspective we want to know how your organization performs through the eyes of your customers and other stakeholders. While financial performance is among the most important metric in terms of an organization's performance, it is not the only one. We also want to know the following:

Does your organization have clearly defined business operations?

Does your organization have clearly defined customer relationship responsibilities for key accounts and an overall customer retention strategy?

Does your organization have a clearly defined profit strategy? (While the terminology may change, this question also applies to non-profit organizations and government agencies).

Do your business operations strategy and customer relations strategy complement your profit strategy?

Are your employees fairly and justly compensated?

Is there a higher-than-normal level of employee turnover or absenteeism within the organization or certain departments? If so, do you know why?

Do you provide employee benefits that are competitive, fair and lucrative to the point that it keeps your best-and-brightest talent from being lured away by the competition?

Does your management set goals that are realistic but also stretch employees to reach beyond their self-imposed limits?

Are your employees recognized and rewarded for their excellent performance based on merit, not entitlement or longevity?

Is your current leadership capable of success? We want to know if your leadership has the proper vision, courage and stamina to undertake tough projects, make difficult decisions, and plow forward when facing criticism and tough odds?

This is the framework we use to assess the strength of your organization's Culture as well as the level of buy-in among your employees, customers, leadership, suppliers and other key stakeholders. Typically, when we find gaps within one or more of the Five Ps, it's a clear indication that your organization is underperforming in that specific area. It can also tell us why you are losing revenue and customers. While assessing your Culture is one of several steps in strengthening your organization's performance and ensuring long-term success, we believe it is among the most important because it reveals the facts according to your most valued stakeholders. We abide by the expression, "Facts are friendly. Sometimes harsh, but always fair!"

By assessing your Culture, you can get your arms around the facts and move forward based on reliable data, information and feedback.

Conscious Business Take-Aways:

1. The key to understanding your Culture from an unbiased perspective is through a comprehensive Culture Assessment.

2. By asking the right questions, your organization will gain a plethora of data, information, knowledge and wisdom. This, in turn, will help your leaders not only make better decisions, but they will make the right decisions the first time!

3. Using the Five Ps of Culture is a proven way to transition from where you are to a balanced or high-performing organization and positively impact your bottom line. Are you ready to raise the bar to reach that level of success?

Chapter 5
The Five Ps of Culture – Purpose

What is the Purpose of a business? The answer to that question has changed radically over the past 30 years. For decades, most business leaders embraced the thinking of economist Milton Friedman who said, "The purpose of a business is to maximize profits for shareholders and owners." That was the key metric for business success. But in the dawn of the 21st Century, the answer has shifted dramatically from profits to people. Today, the primary purpose of a corporation is to serve society and to make the world a better place. In the words of Sam Walton, Founder of Wal-Mart, "There is only one boss and that's the customer. And he/she can fire everybody in the company from the chairman on down simply by spending their money somewhere else." We agree.

Dr. Peter Drucker, the late management guru who inspired a generation of managers and leaders to think beyond the bottom line said, "The goal of every business is the acquisition and maintenance of its customers. Without customers, you're finished." Again, this line of thinking reflects the mindset of a conscious business – putting people first, ahead of profits.

Certainly, value creation and profits are essential to a company's long-term success and viability. This is true for every business and organization whether it operates as a for-profit or a not-for-profit because it takes money to achieve your vision and goals. But ultimately, your business success is determined by your customers and shareholders. In the non-profit world, members or your contributors are the ultimate authority, not the Board of Directors.

When writing this book, we interviewed dozens of executives and leaders who argued strongly that profitability and shareholder primacy were their key metrics. We were reminded repeatedly that these two factors were more important than customer satisfaction because shareholders used one simple measure to evaluate management's performance – the company's stock value. Also, many executives told us they believed shareholders were the "ultimate life force" of their corporation, and if management served the needs of their shareholders, everyone benefits. While it's hard to argue with their logic, we think this line of thinking is seriously flawed because most shareholders care about one thing – Return on Investment (ROI). Certainly, ROI is very important, and that viewpoint is understandable. But from our perspective, it violates the core principle of "people before profits" which is at the heart of a conscious business and *The Heart and Soul of Culture*. Interestingly, not one of them could satisfactorily argue the question: *What happens if you have no customers?* Beyond the obvious answer – you're out of business!

Many leaders also argued that their shareholders were *their* first customers. We heard over and over that shareholder primacy provided management with a "clear sense of direction and definable goals that guide the corporation to do what is good and right." If this were true, corporate blunders like Wells Fargo, Volkswagen, the Takata airbag fiasco, and the BP oil spill in the Gulf of Mexico never would have happened.

Also, in this era of rising stocks and fast profits, shareholder primacy implies short-term decision-making for the sake of generating higher returns and profits. We don't believe that type of thinking should be at the leading edge of management's decision-making process.

Eventually, one question must be asked: *Who are the shareholders' customers?* Isn't the ultimate answer the consumers who buy your company's goods and services? We think so. To take that answer one step further in this era of social consciousness, your customers are also the communities where you build your factories, distribution centers and manufacturing plants. Your customers also include the environment you impact by the way you do business.

The narrow thinking of "profits first" just doesn't play well with the majority of your customers because they aren't consciously concerned with your profitability. Customers care about fair prices, high quality, warranties and reliable service. Your profits are an after-thought to customers. While executives may find that perspective both narrow-minded and insensitive to the company's financial success, it's true. Companies can either deal with that stark reality or run the risk of ignoring their customer's wants and needs. The global graveyard of corporations is filled with companies that never heeded the message of "people before profits" and ultimately failed.

From a corporate Culture perspective, we've been intrigued by Starbucks, a company that has been rightly label the poster child of corporate consciousness. Starbuck's Mission statement is "To inspire and nurture the human spirit – one person, one cup and one neighborhood at a time." Starbuck's Purpose statement is "To establish Starbucks as the premier purveyor of the finest coffee in the world while maintaining our uncompromising principles while we grow." These are lofty goals and reflect visionary thinking on the part of Starbuck's senior leadership, including CEO Kevin Johnson and Howard Schultz, Starbucks' Founder and Chairman emeritus.

Ironically, while Starbucks has been revered for its visionary thinking, the coffee purveyor has also been vilified on several fronts. Among those miscues have been conflicts with various Christian organizations over the Starbuck's holiday cup design. As reporter Liam Stack wrote, "Thanksgiving is right around the corner, which means it is time to embark on a modern American holiday tradition: over-analyzing seasonally available Starbucks cups for signs of liberal nefariousness. Starbucks has produced holiday cups for 20 years. Some have come and gone with little commotion, but others have drawn the ire of conservatives for what some have seen as a secular design scheme that failed to show proper respect for Christianity."

While some, including us, would argue that such criticism is both unfounded and nitpicking, it does prove that a global company like Starbucks must seriously evaluate everything it does vis-a-vis its corporate Mission and Purpose. Starbucks has also had to tip-toe through a minefield of accusations that the company discriminates against certain minorities. The most serious grievance occurred in 2018 when two black men, who were quietly waiting to meet someone at a Philadelphia Starbucks and had not purchased anything, were asked to leave by a Starbucks manager. When the two men refused to leave, police were summoned, and they arrested the two men for trespassing and disturbing the peace.

What happened next was a public relations nightmare for Starbucks as onlookers recorded the two black men being arrested by Philadelphia police. Beyond the negative publicity, the stock market reacted very poorly to Starbucks' decision to close its 8,000 stores for employee training on how to treat customers with respect and dignity as well as a learning session on race, bias and building diversity for the company's 179,000 employees.

It was a costly blunder on the part of one Starbucks manager and it forced Starbucks CEO Kevin Johnson to apologize for the unfortunate incident, stating the company's goal is to do "whatever we can to make things right." Chairman emeritus Howard Schultz commented, "The company's founding values are based on humanity and inclusion. We will learn from our mistakes and reaffirm our commitment to creating a safe and welcoming environment for every customer."

While Starbucks will bounce back from these types of mistakes, it proves our point that it only takes one employee to do something stupid or act outside the cultural boundaries of the organization to cause a major disruption or catastrophe. While closing all its stores was a highly unusual step since most large companies have employees participate in online training during or after business hours, Starbucks' management wanted to demonstrate a more meaningful exercise and selected to close company stores so staff members could have informal meetings to discuss the training topics, review the company's playbook and hold purposeful conversations on the company's standards and how to live them. We think more companies should embrace the Starbucks approach because, frankly, it works, and it sent a very strong message to all employees and customers that Starbucks "walks its talk."

Another culturally responsive step taken by Starbucks was their announcement that the company will open its first American "signing store," a Washington, D.C. store designed to uniquely serve the hearing impaired. The signing store is near Gallaudet University, a 150-year old college for some 1,900 deaf and hard of hearing students located in northeast Washington, D.C. While Starbucks has long been known for its brand dedication, employee-centric Culture and its willingness to think outside the box, this visionary step tells us that Starbucks understands that opening its first USA-based signing store will not only be viewed as a positive step to compliment Starbucks' Mission and Purpose, but it also reaffirms Starbucks' commitment to serving individuals who enjoy coffee but require special needs and services.

Starbucks opened its first signing store in Malaysia in 2016. "Starbucks has always hired the deaf at our stores even before we were planning the signing stores," says Rina Siew, Starbucks corporate Social Responsibility Manager for Malaysia. "However, we could only give them very simple and menial tasks. After a while, we realized that we needed to give them a platform where they could actually thrive, and where we as employers can provide a better partner experience for them."

The Malaysian store's employees, both deaf and hearing, were enrolled in a 10-week sign language course that also highlighted deaf Culture, and the Washington, D.C. store has hired staff who are already fluent in American Sign Language (ASL). Deaf employees will don a special apron embroidered with ASL symbols while hearing employees will sport a pin that identifies their proficiency in sign language. But fluency in ASL is only one piece of the puzzle: The physical space is equally important.

Mark Arnold, of On the Mark Strategies, wrote about Starbucks and three things the coffee giant got right with the signing store. Here's some of what he wrote:

1. Showing Commitment to Employees.

The idea for the signing store actually came from Starbucks' deaf partners (employees) themselves. Starbucks discovered these employees faced workplace limitations and often struggled to excel in the loud, fast-paced corporate environment. Far more than they wanted to reach new customers, Starbucks wanted to better serve its employees.

2. Creating Brand Ambassadors.

In building a signing store, Starbucks created thousands of brand ambassadors within the organization who can uniquely communicate with a segment of the population outside the organization. While all signing store employees (hearing and deaf) will be fluent in American Sign Language, deaf employees will wear specific aprons with sign language symbols. These employees are reaching deaf customers where they are and welcoming them into the Starbucks Culture. But Starbucks isn't just creating brand ambassadors within the organization. Members of the deaf community are also openly supporting the coffee giant.

Howard Rosenblum, CEO of the National Association of the Deaf said, "Starbucks has taken an innovated approach to incorporating Deaf Culture that will increase employment opportunities as well as accessibility for deaf and hard of hearing people, while at the same time educating and enlightening society."

3. Taking Strategic, Mission-driven action.

As we've mentioned, Starbucks' Mission statement is "To inspire and nurture the human spirit – one person, one cup and one neighborhood at a time." The company has consistently strived to emphasize the human aspect of the mission, going out of its way to participate in activist causes. One of their four value statements reads, "Acting with courage, challenging the status quo and finding new ways to grow our company and each other."

While Starbucks' decision to open a signing store in Washington, D.C. was strategic, it wasn't driven by the bottom line. It was driven by a commitment to the company's mission and values. Starbucks didn't just leave their mission and values on the wall. They took steps to put them into action.

This is how you live your brand and allow your Culture to guide you.

In a 2014 HuffPost article, Judith Samuelson, Executive Director at the Aspen Institute's Business and Society Program, wrote "Google, Capitalist Dilemmas and Corporate Purpose: What We Want from Business" Her post supports our argument about Culture and the importance of a company's purpose:

> Google's founders have been clear about the company's purpose: "to organize the world's information and make it universally accessible and useful." This purpose bleeds into the culture of the company and makes Google a pretty fun – and lucrative – place to work. Taking on the challenge of "organizing the world's information" while generating a healthy profit is a good story. And the lesson my faculty friend imparts is an important one: business can be about something truly important – as well as profitable.
>
> This lesson seems to have been lost on a generation of business school graduates who have been steeped in theory and practice aligned with "shareholders first" – or "shareholders only" – as the central organizing principle and primary success metric of a business.

To define your organization's purpose, you should ask three questions:

What is our vision? This question is aspirational in nature. It's a good idea to pose this question every year at your leadership retreat. We also suggest that you ask this question of every employee in your organization because their responses and feedback can be eye-opening and even jaw-dropping!

What do we want our company to become? Just as young people ask this question upon choosing a career, organizations need to do the same. Vision emerges from a sense of purpose. It forms the why, but it also embraces the future as in "how to become" the best, the most respected in our industry, the highest quality producer of goods and/or services or the most trusted.

What is our mission? Very often this is the easiest to answer because all you need to do is look around at what you're doing. Your mission is the *what* of an organization. For example, if you work in a mental health facility, your mission might be to provide the best care for your patients, aid in their healthy recovery, and provide therapy to those who suffer from conditions that inhibit their ability to enjoy a higher quality of life.

What are our values? Neither vision nor mission mean much if they're not reinforced by strong values. Values shape the Culture – that is, the way people behave toward others. Ethics and integrity are a given, but people want more than good behavior. They also want to work in a place where cooperation and collaboration are norms. They want to know their work matters and that they will be recognized for it. Values enforce the behaviors that employees cherish.

We encourage our clients to pose these aforementioned questions to every participant in advance of the company's annual leadership retreat. The responses you'll receive will provide a trove of important answers that you can use to not only measure the thinking of senior management, but also steer the company in new directions.

Conscious Business Take-Aways:

1. Your purpose is paramount to achieving success. As the axiom says, "If you don't know where you're going, any road will take you there." Understanding your Purpose gives you clarity of direction.
2. Purpose cannot be achieved without the continuous drumbeating of leadership, so leadership's anthem must be: who we are, where we're going and how we'll lead you there!
3. Once your Purpose is clear, make sure your employees and suppliers understand it, as well as their role in helping you achieve success.

Chapter 6
The Five Ps of Culture – Principles

Principles are the second of our Five Ps. Principles include a company's core values and its business practices. We believe that core values are at the heart of a company's Culture and those core values should guide the organization's thinking, actions and decisions. Core values should serve as the Culture cornerstone of every organization. It takes time to develop principles, but once they're set, a company's principles should rarely change because this is how employees are trained to think and act, and customers come to know your business and trust you to do right by them.

In 2002, Patrick M. Lencioni, the founder and president of the Table Group, wrote an excellent article that was published in the Harvard Business Review. It was entitled, *Make Your Values Mean Something*. He cautioned CEOs to carefully consider adopting only those core values they can live with. Lencioni wrote, "If you're not willing to accept the pain real values incur, don't bother going to the trouble of formulating a values statement. You'll be better off without one. But if you have the fortitude to see the effort through, you can learn some important lessons from the few companies that have adopted meaningful corporate values.

One textbook example of a company that adopted window-dressing core values was Enron, the Houston-based energy company that went bankrupt in 2002, lost $63 billion and caused 21,000 employees to lose their well-paying jobs. Enshrined on the walls of Enron's corporate headquarters were its core principles:

"Communication. Respect. Integrity and Excellence. Regrettably, these words held no meaning for senior management who lied, cheated and defrauded Enron employees and shareholders. While Enron is an extreme case, Lencioni notes that Enron "is hardly the only company with a hollow set of values." He adds, "Most values statements are bland, toothless, or just plain dishonest. And far from being harmless, as some executives assume, they're often highly destructive. Empty values statements create cynical and dispirited employees, alienate customers, and undermine managerial credibility."

We agree. Your principles should reflect who you are, what your company stands for, and how you treat your employees, suppliers and customers. They should be able to stand the test of time. If a CEO reflects on his/her major decisions, each and every *right* decision can be linked to a core value or principle of the business. While making big decisions is never easy, a leader who makes decisions by weighing his/her options with the core values and principles of the business is rarely wrong.

Too often we read about companies that go astray and lose their cultural compass in terms of doing the right thing. We refer to these companies as Pirate Ships because they are often led by a few tyrannical executives who fully subscribe to Admiral David Farragut's acclaimed order during the Battle of Mobile Bay in 1864 when he shouted, "Damn the torpedoes, full speed ahead!"

In today's complicated and competitive marketplace, very few companies can afford to ignore the torpedoes because it will sink your ship! Furthermore, arrogant leaders are usually poor listeners, or worse, they only listen to yes-men who will support their irrational or ill-conceived plans. We believe this is exactly what happened within Volkswagen and BP Oil. When you have a Captain Jack Sparrow at the helm of a pirate ship organization, two things usually happen. First, he will sail your pirate ship wherever the wind will take him. In other words, there is no "True North" sense of direction. Everything is done by the seat of his/her pants. Your crew (employees) cannot fathom which course to set because the captain's plan is always changing. So why bother, they ask?

Second, you cannot react in time to changing winds. When market conditions change or require a significant shift in your strategy, a pirate ship cannot change its course in time to react to those changes. It's doomed. What eventually happens is the ship's captain forces many of his crew to walk the plank through downsizing and pay cuts. Eventually, the remaining crew will create a mutiny and force the captain to walk his own plank. We see this scenario play out frequently. Just look at Uber, Yahoo!, Hewlett-Packard, Papa John's Pizza and other major companies whose leaders were ousted because of their inability to navigate turbulent seas during tough economic conditions.

Companies that display a strong corporate Culture, including 3M, Google, Apple, Amazon and the Walt Disney Company, typically enjoy higher levels of profitability, customer satisfaction and employee participation. This is also true in the nonprofit sector. St. Jude's Children's Research Hospital, the pediatric research hospital where sick children are often treated at no cost, is a shining example of how an organization's guiding principles can create a positive workplace environment. At St. Jude's, they pride themselves on creating a Culture centered on saving lives and giving hope to thousands of children and their families who are facing life-threatening diseases.

Another example of a nonprofit organization that is true to its mission and core values is the USO (United Service Organizations) which operates more than 200 USO centers at airports and military installations around the world to ensure members of the armed forces stay connected with family, home and country.

At a time when the banking industry has suffered from self-inflicted blunders and bad decisions, Navy Federal Credit Union, the world's largest credit union serving the military and their families, is a good example of how a nonprofit organization can blend its mission, vision and guiding principles to create success. Ranked by Fortune magazine as one of the "top 50 workplaces in America," Navy Federal's employees honor their unwavering commitment to serve America's military and their families through competitive loan rates, easy-to-understand financial products and services, community engagement, and by treating employees with respect. At Navy Federal, management goes to great lengths to ensure its core values of respect, fairness and equality are felt by all who work there. For most employees, it's more than just a job. It's about service to members and making small differences in the lives of their member-customers.

There's a reason why companies like Apple, Amazon, Alphabet (Google's parent company) and Berkshire Hathaway consistently top Fortune's list of Most Admired Companies. Not only are they outstanding performers in their respective industries, but they are known for their principles as much as their ability to generate profits.

When you consider the criteria used by Fortune (and developed by the Hay Group) to determine its list of Most Admired Companies, many of the nine attributes are based on the *quality* of the business and a company's *reputation*, not its profitability. In other words, *people first*. Below are the nine attributes used by Fortune on which companies are evaluated in determining their industry rankings. We think it's a good list and one every CEO should include in his/her strategic plan for success:

1. Ability to attract and retain talented people
2. Quality of management
3. Social responsibility to the community and the environment
4. Innovativeness
5. Quality of products or services
6. Wise use of corporate assets
7. Financial soundness
8. Long-term investment value
9. Effectiveness in doing business globally

In researching the topic of Culture, we examined hundreds of companies to determine what makes them tick. We always asked these questions: Why are these companies so successful? and What core principles appear repeatedly that distinguish these top performers from the rest of the pack? When we put our list together, one company, Alphabet (the parent of Google) encompassed all of the core principles we had listed as part of their Culture.

In an article written by Mary Blackiston, the Content Marketing Specialist for Success agency, she highlights many of Google's core principles and defined each one. Here's what she wrote, in part:

1. Define Core Values.

First and foremost, spell out your company's core values to all employees to make sure that everyone is on the same page. This can help set some parameters to measure both individual and company success. Then when hiring, discuss your company's core values with candidates and ask questions that will help determine if the candidates share those values.

2. Hire Based on Character, Not Skill-Set.

It's reported that Google receives nearly three million job applications per year and only hires about 7,000 of those applicants. So what does this mega-selective company look for in its candidates? In his book, Work Rules, Laszlo Bock explains that they search for people who are fun, intellectually humble, conscientious and comfortable dealing with the unknown. Of the many things that they look for, Google also looks for work ethic more than IQ level. Perhaps surprisingly, they do not really care about GPAs. Remember that skills can be taught. Character, generally, cannot. So find employees that embody the characteristics and values that are most important to you and your company. This approach reminds us of Bruce Nordstrom's famous response when asked how Nordstrom attracts such great employees. He said, "We hire the smile and train the skill."

3. Don't Be a Copycat.

Google allows its employees to bring their dogs to work. Is this normal for such a massive organization? Certainly not, but that doesn't mean it shouldn't be done. A forward-thinking, innovative mentality is essential to business growth and longevity. So don't just copy what other companies do. Try things out. Determine what works best for your business and what type of culture will make *your* employees happiest.

4. Embrace Transparency.

At Google, employees are encouraged to ask questions and speak their minds. According to one Googler, "My mentor created psychological safety for me on my first day when he said, "Don't be afraid to ask questions – you don't have to impress me. You already have, and that's why I hired you."

Strive to establish and maintain a culture of open and honest communication. Provide and seek constructive feedback on a regular basis. Instead of guessing, ask questions if you're unsure about something. Not happy with a colleague or a situation? Speak up. Made a big mistake? Instead of hiding the evidence or shifting the blame, own up to it. Transparency from the top to the bottom is key to any successful business.

CEOs and leaders should not be afraid to admit when they are wrong or if they don't know the answer to something. Being a great leader is, in large part, about honesty and humility. The more honest a leader is, the more trust and loyalty employees will have in both the leader and the company. The trickle effect is also very powerful. If leaders of a company are transparent, more likely than not their subordinates will be as well.

5. Allow for Some Fun.

Between Google's volleyball courts, basketball courts and bowling alleys, there is never a shortage of activities for employees to engage in outside of the office. But don't be fooled – there are ways to create a great company culture without spending a ton of money or supplying lots of cool gadgets.

If you're location-based, this could be designating one room as the "play room," filled with comfortable chairs, books, board games and the like. You could also hold monthly office competitions. Get your team outside of the office every now and then and go on a hike – or maybe hold a scavenger hunt downtown.

If you're a remote-based team, you will obviously have to find more intangible ways to have a good time. It could be as simple as taking some time out from a video meeting to discuss everyone's favorite TV shows or books. Slack, the messaging application, is our virtual office. This is where we will occasionally share photos of our daily lives and funny GIFs with one another throughout the day.

Another remote-based team has mid-week "happy hours," where employees will get together via video chat and discuss things unrelated to work – often with a beverage in hand, of course!

The point is not what you do or where you do it – what matters is that team members get to know one another and bond outside of the office setting. The better team members get along with one another, the happier and more productive they will be when they are at work.

6. Create Shared Leadership.

Google is also known for its start-up mentality and flat organizational structure, which means that there are few or no levels of middle management. In other words, despite its massive size, all employees have the opportunity to lead.

Create shared leadership at your company by letting each team member take the initiative and be a leader, even if it's just once a month. In meetings, people in upper management roles should not be the only ones talking. Make sure everyone has a chance to contribute.

7. Be Open to Change.

The flat organizational structure that Google is renowned for encourages all employees to speak-up and vocalize their points of view. This means that if a lower-level employee has an opinion about something, he or she can bypass middle management and go straight to the CEO.

Of course, not every company has to adopt the same organizational structure. What matters is remaining open to change, however that may be. Once a company becomes set in its ways, it is much harder to make amendments and evolve down the line.

Allow your business to prosper by prioritizing the continual advancement of your company and employees. As a leader, this means not only being open to new ideas but also encouraging them. It means examining the processes and procedures that are currently in place and wondering how they can be improved upon. As an employee, this means not being afraid to make your voice heard.

Final Words:

As Google co-founder, Larry Page, said, "At the end of the day, it's important that the company be a family, that people feel that they're part of the company, and that the company is like a family to them. When you treat people that way, you get better productivity." You also get success!

What's noteworthy is that Google's vision for success is not about the short-term. Its founders, Larry Page and Sergey Brin, wrote the following in their initial public offering letter in 2004:

"Our goal is to develop services that significantly improve the lives of as many people as possible. In pursuing this goal, we may do things that we believe have a positive impact on the world, even if the near-term financial returns are not obvious. For example, we make our services as widely available as we can by supporting over 90 languages and by providing most services for free. Advertising is our principal source of revenue, and the ads we provide are relevant and useful rather than intrusive and annoying. We strive to provide users with great commercial information."

"We are proud of the products we have built, and we hope that those we create in the future will have an even greater positive impact on the world."

"As a private company, we have concentrated on the long term, and this has served us well. As a public company, we will do the same. In our opinion, outside pressures too often tempt companies to sacrifice long term opportunities to meet quarterly market expectations. Sometimes this pressure has caused companies to manipulate financial results in order to "make their quarter." In Warren Buffett's words, 'We won't 'smooth' quarterly or annual results: If earnings figures are lumpy when they reach headquarters, they will be lumpy when they reach you.'"

We were intrigued by Google's commitment to the long-term view instead of focusing on their quarterly earnings. We were also impressed by other core principles that distinguished Google from most other companies. At the heart of Google's core principles is a simple document written by Google co-founders Larry Page and Sergey Brin entitled, *Ten Things We Know to Be True*. In this document they lay out their personal philosophy and set the standard for all who follow. Here it is:

Ten Things We Know to Be True: **by Larry Page and Sergey Brin**
We first wrote these "10 things" when Google was just a few years old. From time to time we revisit this list to see if it still holds true. We hope it does – and you can hold us to that.

1. Focus on the user and all else will follow.
Since the beginning, we've focused on providing the best user experience possible. Whether we're designing a new Internet browser or a new tweak to the look of the homepage, we take great care to ensure that they will ultimately serve you, rather than our own internal goal or bottom line. Our homepage interface is clear and simple, and pages load instantly. Placement in search results is never sold to anyone, and advertising is not only clearly marked as such, it offers

relevant content and is not distracting. And when we build new tools and applications, we believe they should work so well you don't have to consider how they might have been designed differently.

2. It's best to do one thing really, really well.

We do search. With one of the world's largest research groups focused exclusively on solving search problems, we know what we do well, and how we could do it better. Through continued iteration on difficult problems, we've been able to solve complex issues and provide continuous improvements to a service that already makes finding information a fast and seamless experience for millions of people. Our dedication to improving search helps us apply what we've learned to new products, like Gmail and Google Maps. Our hope is to bring the power of search to previously unexplored areas, and to help people access and use even more of the ever-expanding information in their lives.

3. Fast is better than slow.

We know your time is valuable, so when you're seeking an answer on the web you want it right away – and we aim to please. We may be the only people in the world who can say our goal is to have people leave our website as quickly as possible. By shaving excess bits and bytes from our pages and increasing the efficiency of our serving environment, we've broken our own speed records many times over, so that the average response time on a search result is a fraction of a second. We keep speed in mind with each new product we release, whether it's a mobile application or Google Chrome, a browser designed to be fast enough for the modern web. And we continue to work on making it all go even faster.

4. Democracy on the web works.

Google search works because it relies on the millions of individuals posting links on websites to help determine which other sites offer content of value. We assess the importance of every web page using more than 200 signals and a variety of techniques, including our patented PageRank™ algorithm, which analyzes which sites have been "voted" to be the best sources of information by other pages across the web. As the web gets bigger, this approach actually improves, as each new site is another point of information and another vote to be counted. In the same vein, we are active in open source software development, where innovation takes place through the collective effort of many programmers.

5. You don't need to be at your desk to need an answer.

The world is increasingly mobile: people want access to information wherever they are, whenever they need it. We're pioneering new technologies and offering new solutions for mobile services that help people all over the globe to do any number of tasks on their phone, from checking email and calendar events to watching videos, not to mention the several different ways to access Google search on a phone. In addition, we're hoping to fuel greater innovation for mobile users everywhere with Android, a free, open source mobile platform. Android brings the openness that shaped the Internet to the mobile world. Not only does Android benefit consumers, who have more choice and innovative new mobile experiences, but it opens up revenue opportunities for carriers, manufacturers and developers.

6. You can make money without doing evil.

Google is a business. The revenue we generate is derived from offering search technology to companies and from the sale of advertising displayed on our site and on other sites across the web. Hundreds of thousands of advertisers worldwide use AdWords to promote their products; hundreds of thousands of publishers take advantage of our AdSense program to deliver ads relevant to their site content. To ensure that we're ultimately serving all our users (whether they are advertisers or not), we have a set of guiding principles for our advertising programs and practices:

A. We don't allow ads to be displayed on our results pages unless they are relevant where they are shown. And we firmly believe that ads can provide useful information if, and only if, they are relevant to what you wish to find – so it's possible that certain searches won't lead to any ads at all.

B. We believe that advertising can be effective without being flashy. We don't accept pop-up advertising, which interferes with your ability to see the content you've requested. We've found that text ads that are relevant to the person reading them draw much higher clickthrough rates than ads appearing randomly. Any advertiser, whether small or large, can take advantage of this highly targeted medium.

C. Advertising on Google is always clearly identified as a "Sponsored Link," so it does not compromise the integrity of our search results. We never manipulate rankings to put our partners higher in our search results and no one can buy better PageRank. Our users trust our objectivity and no short-term gain could ever justify breaching that trust.

7. There's always more information out there.

Once we'd indexed more of the HTML pages on the Internet than any other search service, our engineers turned their attention to information that was not as readily accessible. Sometimes it was just a matter of integrating new databases into search, such as adding a phone number and address lookup and a business directory. Other efforts required a bit more creativity, like adding the ability to search news archives, patents, academic journals, billions of images and millions of books. And our researchers continue looking into ways to bring all the world's information to people seeking answers.

8. The need for information crosses all borders.

Our company was founded in California, but our mission is to facilitate access to information for the entire world, and in every language. To that end, we have offices in more than 60 countries, maintain more than 180 Internet domains, and serve more than half of our results to people living outside the United States. We offer Google's search interface in more than 130 languages, offer people the ability to restrict results to content written in their own language, and aim to provide the rest of our applications and products in as many languages and accessible formats as possible. Using our translation tools, people can discover content written on the other side of the world in languages they don't speak. With these tools and the help of volunteer translators, we have been able to greatly improve both the variety and quality of services we can offer in even the most far-flung corners of the globe.

9. You can be serious without a suit.

We built Google around the idea that work should be challenging, and the challenge should be fun. We believe that great, creative things are more likely to happen with the right company culture – and that doesn't just mean lava lamps and rubber balls. There is an emphasis on team achievements and pride in individual accomplishments that contribute to our overall success. We put great stock in our employees – energetic, passionate people from diverse backgrounds with creative approaches to work, play and life. Our atmosphere may be casual, but as new ideas emerge in a café line, at a team meeting or at the gym, they are traded, tested and put into practice with dizzying speed – and they may be the launch pad for a new project destined for worldwide use.

10. Great just isn't good enough.

We see being great at something as a starting point, not an endpoint. We set ourselves goals we know we can't reach yet, because we know that by stretching to meet them, we can get further than we expected. Through innovation and iteration, we aim to take things that work well and improve upon them in unexpected ways. For example, when one of our engineers saw that search worked well for properly spelled words, he wondered about how it handled typos. That led him to create an intuitive and more helpful spell checker.

Even if you don't know exactly what you're looking for, finding an answer on the web is our problem, not yours. We try to anticipate needs not yet articulated by our global audience and meet them with products and services that set new standards. When we launched Gmail, it had more storage space than any email service available. In retrospect, offering that seems obvious – but that's because now we have new standards for email storage. Those are the kinds of changes we seek to make, and we're always looking for new places where we can make a difference. Ultimately, our constant dissatisfaction with the way things are becomes the driving force behind everything we do.

Conscious Business Take-Aways:

1. Your Principles define your Culture. It's the leader's responsibility to establish the organization's core principles and exhibit those principles on a consistent, daily basis. This is ultimately why leadership is so difficult. It's hard to "walk the talk" every day.

2. There should be no gray areas when it comes to upholding and enforcing your core principles. Every employee should know them, and every employee should be expected to adhere to the organization's core principles.

3. Use a Culture Assessment to determine if your employees know the organization's core principles and how committed they are to honoring these same principles.

Chapter 7
The Five Ps of Culture – People

We have always believed in putting people ahead of profits. Our rationale is simple. We believe that if you hire the right people, train and empower them to do their job and recognize them for meeting or exceeding your expectations, you will generate more profits. Obviously, other factors come into play, such as a providing your customers with a quality product or service and controlling expenses. But in the final analysis, your customer relationships – and their decision to buy your products or services – are in the hands of your employees.

Here are three trivial yet important examples of how employees impact sales through customer relations. For lunch, we frequently go around the corner from our office in San Diego to a Subway sandwich shop. It's one of four fast food choices we have nearby. When we walk in there's usually a line of customers waiting to place their orders, but as soon as we enter the small sub shop, a friendly employee voice calls out, "Welcome to Subway. We'll be with you in just a moment!" Trivial? Yes. Insignificant? No! Frankly, it puts us at ease and takes our minds off wondering how long it will take to get a carry out order. Acknowledging and welcoming your customer is so important in creating a great customer experience.

The second example is the proactive customer service that we always experience at Nordstrom. In an era of fierce competition from other retailers and the ease of online shopping, it's always nice to encounter a friendly Nordstrom employee. We were recently shopping at a Nordstrom and were standing by the escalator, looking at the directory to find the location for their customer service department when a Nordstrom employee approached us and asked, "Can I help you find something?" Trivial? Yes. Insignificant? No! Interestingly, she didn't wear a nametag (Nordstrom employees only started wearing nametags in 2017), but it was obvious she worked at the store and was trained to activate her third eye and inner-ear to identify customers in need.

Speaking of activating your employees' third eye and inner-ear, the only airline we've ever flown that possesses this same customer service level is Singapore Airlines. Why is that? We think it has more to do with a Culture of service than anything else. For example, we've never seen Singapore Airline's flight attendants huddled together in the back of the airplane checking their text messages and emails during a flight. At Singapore Airlines, they're always on duty, ready to respond to a passenger's needs. If they take breaks, they do it in private and not in the presence of their passengers. Trivial? Yes. Insignificant? No! It sends a message about their Culture of excellent service and a caring attitude.

By creating a Culture that puts people first, you are sending a signal to your employees, customers and suppliers that they matter. In this technology-driven era where Millennials and Gen Z'ers – your workforce of the future – are more interested in their quality of life than they are in the profitability of your business, it makes smart business sense to shape your Culture around their wants and needs instead of solely focusing on your bottom line. Frankly, this is the direction conscious companies are moving toward because they understand it creates sales and profits!

Of course, profits matter. And yes, you need to be prudent when it comes to spending money. We have witnessed too many companies that have suffered hard times because they didn't follow our basic credo of putting people first and entrusting them with the success of building long-term customer relationships. When a company commits to the People First ideology, it triggers related decisions that will ultimately strengthen your bottom line. For example, companies that adopt the People First philosophy also provide their employees with the training, tools and resources they need to achieve positive results. They form teams to tap into the strengths and talents of their employees, and in so doing, ensure stronger results by creating a competitive and friendly spirit within the organization. They review and remove policies, rules and procedures that inhibit performance or restrict employees from achieving superior results. Yes, they pay their people above average wages and incentivize them with contests, bonuses and other rewards that tell employees "management cares about you" and "thanks for doing a great job!" As one executive from 3M told us a few years ago, "This is not rocket science. Basically, it boils down to common sense and a prudent business management practice."

Recently, we had a client tell us something so simple, and yet it was quite profound. She was commiserating about the lack of productivity at her company's product development division. The company was behind schedule in developing and perfecting the next generation of a high-tech product and as the division Vice President, she was taking heat from the company's senior executives for her team's lack of progress and her inability to meet deadlines. That's why we were brought in.

At our opening interview she said, "You know, we don't hire bad people!" At first we had to let that statement sink in. But as we reflected on it, we discovered not only was she right – we've never met a manager who intentionally hires bad people – but, we realized she was the problem. This vice president had excellent management skills but no connection to her heart skills. Our confidential interviews with over 50 of her employees validated our suspicions. Fortunately, this vice president was coachable and receptive to finding ways to get closer to her people. And she listened! Within three weeks after we started working with her, employees were re-engaged and re-invigorated. They were communicating with each other and suggesting innovative ideas to enhance the product design and mechanics – some suggestions made sense and others didn't, but no one was punished for offering an idea, even if it was an off-the-wall suggestion!

What changed? The vice president changed. With some coaching from us, she found her heart. She realized that her people not only needed to be managed, they also needed to be appreciated, encouraged and challenged. Most important, she included them in the big picture. It's like the old story about the two bricklayers who were asked by a passerby what they were working on as a new church was being constructed. One answered he was merely building a retaining wall while the other said he was building a majestic cathedral. This vice president inspired her team by giving them the big picture of how their product would revolutionize not only their company but help people communicate globally. Who wouldn't want to be part of that inspiring vision? Everybody signed on and did their part to make it happen.

People come in all sizes, shapes, colors, ethnicities and backgrounds. But everyone has a heart, and at the end of the day, everyone wants to be appreciated and know that his/her work makes a difference. Everyone wants to be valued. The senior leadership at companies like Google, 3M, Navy Federal Credit Union, Sharp Healthcare, and other top performers get this.

Unfortunately, while most companies understand this fact, few companies practice it. It's not that management is bad, but rather they are unconscious. When we talk about unconscious companies versus conscious companies, how you treat your people – employees, customers and suppliers – is the differential. If you allow policies, rules and procedures to limit your employees' innovative spirit and ability to have fun in the workplace, you are limiting your company's success. If you create restrictive practices that make it difficult for your customers to do business with you, they will leave. If you don't respect and value your suppliers, they will not be committed to your success, deadlines and requests.

Perhaps this explains Southwest Airlines' secret to being consistently profitable. Yes, while Southwest Airlines has its share of challenges and problems, we can tell you that dedicated employees isn't one of them!

We find that most airlines – with the exception of Southwest Airlines – typically punish their customers when it comes to booking flights or making changes without a severe and costly penalty. Their website and rules for changing tickets are easy to use and favor the customer. Look at how easy Southwest Airlines makes it to book a flight online or change a ticket. Is your company or organization overly complicating life for its customers with punitive policies, rules and procedures? What does it cost you to enforce all of your antiquated and customer-unfriendly policies, rules and procedures? Why not make it easy to do business with you and win more customers while reducing your costs?

When we talk about having fun in the workplace, let's be clear. We are not talking about tolerating misbehavior, sexual harassment or any other kind of deviant behavior. But we are talking about creating a relaxed, energetic and competitive work environment that encourages results and allows your employees to interact professionally and collegially with each other. Yes, management needs to manage, but equally important, management needs to be the bulldozers who clear the way for the team's success. What we have found in too many companies is that management sees its role as a steamroller rather than a bulldozer. Instead of clearing the way for innovation, creativity, harmony, teamwork and fun in the workplace, management is making more rules and policies that inhibit employees from giving 100 percent.

Examine your company's management composition. Do you have steamrollers or bulldozers? Perhaps, if you have too many steamrollers, that's why your employees are under-performing, disengaged, and your company falls into the *Volatile Culture* or *Under-Performing Culture* quadrants.

We've also seen companies rise and fall on the reputation of its leaders. On the positive side, Sir Richard Branson has been a role model and inspiration not only to thousands of Virgin employees, but also entrepreneurs and other CEOs around the world who have followed his guiding principles of putting people ahead of profits and applying the Golden Rule throughout his many companies and ventures, including those that failed.

On the negative side of that equation, you have pompous leaders like John Schnatter, the former chairman and public face of Papa John's pizza chain, who committed a series of blunders when he blamed slow pizza sales on the National Football League's handling of black football players kneeling during the National Anthem. Schnatter was forced out of his chairmanship role at Papa John's in July 2018 when he made a racial slur – using the "N" word – during a conference call that, ironically, was held to boost his image and help him avoid public relations blunders. This caused the pizza chain to retreat to its crisis management bunker and regroup in order to figure out how the company could regain the trust and business of many lost customers, especially among the minority community who were deeply offended by Papa John Schnatter's distasteful comments.

In the end, consumers usually win by protesting or boycotting a brand, or bringing a company's misdeeds to the media forefront. This was the case with Martin Shkreli, the boyish-looking pharmaceutical entrepreneur who caused a public outcry after he drastically raised the price of a life-saving prescription drug, Daraprim, from $13.50 per tablet to $750 a tablet! Despite the public outcry, including negative media profiles on 60 Minutes, Shkreli thumbed his nose at consumers and said his company was doing the right thing. But Shkreli's smug attitude didn't win any points with consumers or U.S. prosecutors. When federal prosecutors looked more closely at his past, they uncovered Shkreli's involvement in what they said was a Ponzi-like scheme at his former hedge fund and a pharmaceutical company he previously headed. Shkreli was charged with fraud, convicted and sent to prison for seven years. The sentencing judge was not lenient.

There's one other area that is a pet peeve of ours when it comes to people. Too often we hear from a client that John or Jane Doe, a valued member of their corporate team, is leaving the company and taking another job that pays more money and has a more important title. In our minds, there's nothing worse than a company losing a good employee because management is unwilling to match the offer. Frankly, in most cases it's a poor business decision to lose a highly-valued employee over a few thousand dollars. It makes no sense when you consider the worth of that high-performer to your organization and the cost of replacing him or her with someone new who has less experience and, perhaps, less talent. Human resources experts tell us that for every $50,000 you pay someone, it will cost you at least 20% to recruit and replace that individual, let alone make up the lost revenue while his/her replacement learns the ropes. We strongly encourage our clients to hold onto their best-and-brightest talent, especially in a tight labor market where good people are hard to find, and the top performers are in high demand. Whenever you give a performance review, make sure there's some money or added benefits put on the table to keep your top performers happy. If you don't do this, they will leave. Trust us – we see it happen every day and you will kick yourself for letting it happen! By the way, it also causes a dip in employee morale and opens the door to other top performers leaving because you can bet your bottom dollar that John or Jane Doe is going to recruit their friends from your company to join them at their new place of employment!

One of the best ways to retain employees is to make certain that their jobs are satisfying to them. We have found a way to bring greater satisfaction into the job experience by introducing the Core Power System to the employee. The Core Power System is designed to help employees see their true potential through their own unique arrangement of eight life skills we call "Core Powers." When employees are connected to their core powers and they are using them in their work, we have found that job satisfaction increases exponentially. The eight Core Powers are inherent to everyone and when we know them and use them, we feel empowered. Empowered employees are happy and engaged.

In Chapter 13, Conscious Business Tools, we discuss in greater detail the Core Power System and its benefits to your employees and company.

Conscious Business Take-Aways:

1. It's no secret that your people are your greatest asset. Do your employees know this through the actions of their leaders?
2. If you are losing a higher-than-normal rate of good talent or customers, have you asked why? Are you altering your policies, rules and procedures to keep your best-and-brightest talent?
3. How does your organization demonstrate that it values and respects its customers?
4. Does your organization's policies, rules and procedures favor the customer or punish them? Do you make it difficult to do business with your company?

Chapter 8

The Five Ps of Culture – Processes

There's an important correlation between Culture and your processes. One reason is that management typically adopts processes that align with their company's Culture and values. While Culture is more of a subconscious nuance in business, factoring Culture into your business processes should not be an unconscious act. Shifting a company's Culture can become a challenge as business conditions change and markets realign to your customers' wants and needs. When this occurs, a company's Culture should shift. And so should your processes.

Because most people are resistant to change, processes can also become outdated or stagnant. This is why it's imperative to monitor your Culture. As the world shifts and markets change, so too must your processes. You cannot continue to manufacture buggy whips when everyone wants to buy a Tesla.

Here's an example of an antiquated process that makes no sense to us. It deals with a respected airline, Qantas, and their apparel rules for passengers using the airline's Business Lounge. Joanne Catherall, a singer with the pop music band Human League, was denied access to the Melbourne Airport's Qantas Business Lounge for wearing Ugg boots. She was told the boots were considered sleepwear. In fact, we are told Qantas specifically cites the Ugg brand in their Business Class Lounge rules and regulations as forbidden apparel. What strikes us as ridiculous is the fact that

Uggs is not only an Australian product, it is probably the one brand most associated with Australia by fashion experts around the world. Second, any intelligent person would know that people do not sleep in their Ugg boots. So for Qantas to continue to ban business class passengers from entering their lounges because they are wearing a pricey fashion item (Uggs are not cheap!) borders on the ridiculous. When Qantas confirmed its policies to us, all we could do was shake our heads in disbelief. We were so shocked by their response that we failed to ask if blue jeans were forbidden, especially the expensive style with holes in the knees and thighs? These are the kind of bonehead rules that make senior management look stupid and only embarrass employees who are required to enforce such draconian policies. Of course, bad policies and rules such as the Qantas-Ugg blooper don't help a company's public relations image or customer retention efforts. Perhaps they forget that customers have choices and bad publicity certainly influences their choices. By the way, we checked Joanne Catherall's Facebook account to see how many followers she had. I'm sure if Qantas knew about the thousands of fans who follow the Human League's singer, they might have thought twice about refusing her entry to their Business Lounge.

Here's a quick exercise that reinforces this point about stagnant processes and Culture shifts. Consider your commute to work. If you drive to work, do you always take the same roads? If you take the train or subway, do you vary your routes? The answer from most people is no, you don't. Another question. While many of our great-grandparents walked to work or rode a bicycle, do you? Probably not. Why not? Because mass transit is faster, cheaper and more reliable.

As times change, so do people and, therefore, so must our processes. We take the same route to work or dress the same way each morning because we are creatures of habit. While there's nothing wrong with driving the same route to work or getting dressed the same way every morning, the rules change when it comes to meeting your customers' needs and expectations. Why? Because times change, and the world has changed, and products change based on the wants and needs of your consumers.

Today's consumers want different things. Think about that great advertising tagline from Oldsmobile in 1989 – "It's not your father's Oldsmobile!" While it was a memorable slogan, it wasn't enough to save the brand because consumers didn't want the same old, same old. They wanted something new and exciting in a car.

Speaking of cars, does anybody you know drive the same old clunker they did 20 years ago? Okay, maybe a few people drive a classic Mustang or Corvette, but the overwhelming majority of us drive a newer model car because we want all the bells and whistles that come with a new car including advanced safety features and updated technology. Interestingly, one survey reveals that Millennials are more interested in the technology features in a new car than what's under the hood. Who would have ever thought auto buyers would be influenced more by the technology in the car than the auto design or horsepower?

In 1987, the Malcolm Baldrige Award was created at a time when foreign competition was outperforming American companies in most industries. The Baldrige Award was designed to help American manufacturers examine their quality and work systems to make them more competitive and successful. A major component of the Baldrige Award, which was named after the late Secretary of Commerce who championed the idea of quality and excellence in business, is a company's work processes.

The Baldrige framework uses a systems approach that helps companies and organizations manage all their components as a unified whole. In other words, to be effective and profitable, your plans, processes, measures and actions must be consistently excellent, not just good.

When we use the term *Processes*, we want to know this: *How do you do what you do? Can you do it faster, better and more economically?* This question is at the heart of the Baldrige Award criteria and it certainly should be at the heart of your Culture strategy. We define a work process as a series of vital steps that are performed by a work team to achieve a specific goal. These steps – or work processes – are typically repeated many times, sometimes by multiple users, and ideally in a standardized and optimized way.

As more companies and organizations transition from manual processes to automated processes, the role of technology has become very important because it supports the work team or users in implementing the work process in a more accurate, standardized and optimized manner. In the late 1980s, flowcharts, dashboards, Six Sigma and other business process management tools were introduced to help companies streamline their work processes to be more competitive. Many of those same tools are being used today to give progressive companies an advantage over their competition in many areas ranging from manufacturing and finance to risk management and compliance. Also, as a result of companies focusing on processes, major strides have been made in departmental functions such as budgeting, receiving orders, invoicing, shipping products, supply chain management, human resources, data security, updating employee information, and sales/marketing.

From a Culture perspective, processes are critical to your company's sustainability and growth because every successful company and organization must measure, analyze and manage its key functions, resources and people to create better efficiency. This is how businesses stay competitive and relevant in a global economy.

As we go to print, Boeing, the airplane manufacturer, is struggling to answer questions about its processes relating to its new Boeing 737 Max jet. Following two eerily similar tragic crashes of the new airplanes in Indonesia and Ethiopia that together killed 346 people, investigators and regulators think the crashes were caused in part by a malfunctioning automated system – and the pilots' lack of training around how to deal with it – that was designed to keep the aircraft from stalling in flight. Similarities between the crashes, and the log of complaints from other pilots about the system in question, all point to trouble with the Maneuvering Characteristics Augmentation System, or MCAS.

These concerns beg the question about what processes Boeing used to design the sophisticated MCAS, and what training pilots received to operate the new aircraft and the MCAS. As more information is revealed, it appears that Boeing and the Federal Aviation Administration (FAA) agreed to limit pilot training on the new 737 Max jet to 56 minutes using only an iPad. Was this adequate training? According to several pilots who flew the plane and the pilots' union, the crew was not adequately informed on how to operate or override the MCAS. This could explain why two 737 Max jets crashed; the pilots didn't know how to override the MCAS when it malfunctioned.

What is troubling to us from a Process perspective are the following questions:

1. Did Boeing try to save money by limiting crew training on the new airplane to a 56-minute iPad course? If so, this raises several related questions about why Boeing would put profits before safety. If this was the case, it causes us to wonder about Boeing's guiding principles, and who within

the company was responsible for managing risks and protecting the company against reputational loss?

2. Did the FAA turn a blind eye to Boeing's training processes on the new airplane and simply trust Boeing to provide adequate training to pilots flying the new 737 Max jet?

3. Did the FAA expedite approval of the new MACS technology without thoroughly investigating the design and functionality?

When you consider that Boeing (and other airplane manufacturers) have embraced a self-regulating posture because the FAA is grossly understaffed and, therefore, unable to inspect and evaluate all aspects of a new airplane's design, it creates a very risky scenario that a leading aviation safety forecasting group has warned of for over a decade.

In 2004, the Future Aviation Safety Team (FAST), a group first convened in 1999 by a consortium of international flight regulators and co-chaired by Brian E. Smith of NASA Ames Research Center, published a report on "Increasing Reliance on Flight Deck Automation" – a trend that was already underway. According to FAST, the report had two main conclusions:

a) that there will be problems with maintaining "hands-on" currency due to future advances in flight deck automation, and,

b) that human stress and fatigue will increase rapidly when the flight crew do not understand what flight deck automation is asking the aircraft to do.

The report used the term "automation surprise," and it accurately describes what might have happened to the pilots attempting to overcome the MCAS system to keep their Boeing Max planes from crashing.

While commercial airplane crashes generate sensational news headlines because of the large loss of life, this tragic scenario is a good example of how a broken process can seriously damage a company's bottom line as well as cause unforeseen reputational risk.

On a smaller scale, consider what would happen if Intel tried to develop a new processor for computers without mastering and beta testing all its processes. This is why every department in your company must have refined processes if that department is going to function at its peak level.

We only need to look at Amazon as an example of how one company mastered its work processes to not only transform the world of selling books but a wide range of products and services that consumers desire. When you realize the scope and magnitude of its operations – from placing products on its website to order fulfillment, what Amazon has accomplished in terms of process management is rather incredible although they are far from finished. Today, Amazon is using technology to create delivery drones and driverless cars. Can you imagine what our highways will look like in twenty years as driverless cars and trucks take to the interstates and freeways of the world? Also, every truck driver, Uber and Lyft driver should be concerned about his/her job because technology will render those professions obsolete in 25 years. This is how work processes impact not only your business but an entire industry and nation.

There are ten core work processes we encourage every business to examine as part of its Culture Assessment. They are described in the chart below which was developed by Bizmanualz, an excellent company established in 1995 that offers a complete line of MS-Word company policies, procedures and forms templates for key business functions and processes.

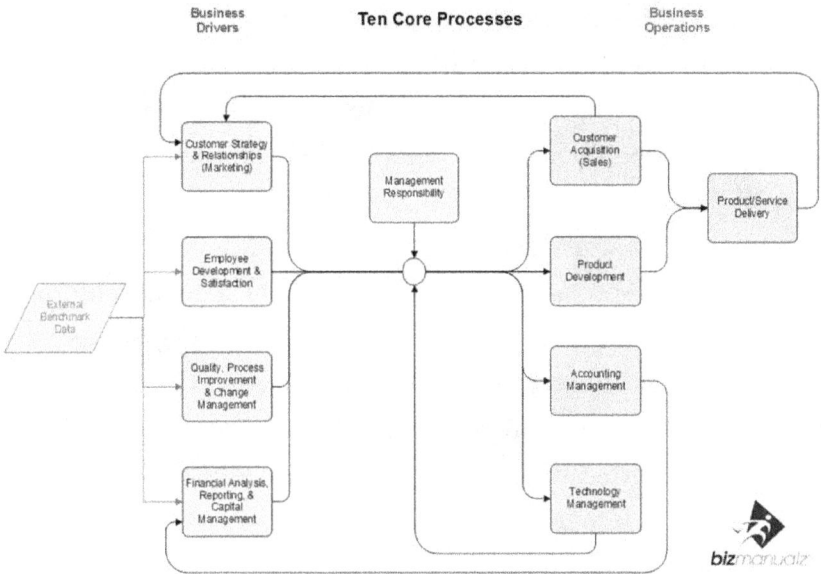

When we conduct a Culture Assessment, these are the same ten processes we examine. Typically, most issues relating to performance and profitability are found somewhere in one or more of these ten areas because these areas represent the heart and soul of a business – and therefore, the heart and soul of its Culture.

Sometime a company can get cross-wired and disregard both its Culture and processes when making major decisions. Earlier in our book, we discussed the depraved decision by Volkswagen when the automaker based in Wolfsburg, Germany intentionally programmed turbocharged direct injection (TDI) diesel engines to activate their emissions controls only during laboratory emissions testing. This rigging of the TDI caused the vehicles to meet EPA standards, but when the vehicles weren't being tested, they emitted up to 40 times more nitrogen oxide emissions on the open highways. When sued by the U.S. government and the state of California, Volkswagen admitted that they had implemented this programming software in nearly eleven million cars worldwide, and 500,000 in the United States, in model years 2009 through 2015. The United States Justice Department said that in 2006 VW realized it could not meet the tougher rules implemented by the EPA, so VW engineers designed a system to detect when cars were being tested in the lab.

This criminal act eventually cost Volkswagen $4.3 billion in fines plus the $158.3 million it had to pay to the state of California to settle its lawsuit against VW. Additionally, Volkswagen agreed to spend up to $22 billion in the United States to address claims from owners, environmental regulators, other states and its dealers. Ouch! With reported sales of $258.5 billion in 2017, that total sum is still a significant bite from their bottom line.

Also, six executives from Volkswagen were indicted on criminal charges and await their fate as we go to print. Among those indicted was Heinz-Jakob Neusser, former head of development for VW Brand, who was suspended in 2015 and previously the head of engine development. Two other former heads of engine development, Jens Hadler and Richard Dorenkamp, were also indicted.

We mention these individuals because this was not the irresponsible act of one or two persons, but rather, it required a criminal conspiracy of numerous VW employees, all of whom went along with a half-baked scheme; and not one person amongst them had the guts to challenge the warped thinking of its leadership at the time. This is what we mean when we talk about a broken process and ignoring the important alignment between Culture and processes. What Volkswagen perpetrated didn't happen on the assembly line. It happened in the conference rooms and executive suites at Volkswagen's headquarters where intelligence and common sense should have prevailed.

"It is now clear that Volkswagen's top executives knew about this illegal activity and deliberately kept regulators, shareholders and consumers in the dark – and they did this for years," said Andrew McCabe, the FBI's deputy director, at a press conference. "We can't put companies in jail, but we can hold their employees personally accountable. And we can force companies to pay hefty fines."

So these are the facts. But the questions we continue to ask ourselves from a process standpoint are this: How did this happen in a company that enjoyed a solid reputation, strong profits and was widely respected as a model of excellence in the automotive industry? And why did the conspiracy continue for nearly eight years with dozens of employees knowing it was illegal, morally deceptive, and violated the company's guiding principles? Why did no one at Volkswagen have the courage or guts to challenge this irrational action that violated the company's processes? Interestingly, to this day, no employee at Volkswagen has come forward to tell the whole story. This fact also says something about the company's Culture, and it is not positive.

We can only surmise that senior management panicked when they realized they could not meet the EPA's rigid new standards for emissions. Instead of seeking a reasonable delay through legal channels or devising new technology to fix the problem, management got greedy, stupid, and strayed from its Culture roots all at the same time. As strange as that sounds, they wouldn't be the first senior management team to do so. Nevertheless, it was arrogant on the part of Volkswagen's senior leadership to ever think they could get away with reprogramming the TDIs and nobody would notice. A broken process squeaks just as loudly on the showroom floor as it does on the assembly line!

For nearly eight years they perpetrated their criminal act. Eventually, a small research team led by Mr. Dan Carder at the University of West Virginia's Center for Fuels, Engines and Emissions, discovered serious discrepancies in VW's diesel emissions. I'm sure Volkswagen had never heard of this tiny research center, let alone figured it would unmask VW's brilliant emissions software adjustments. Unfortunately, it wasn't so brilliant after all!

We live in a world where everyone has a cell phone, everyone has a camera or a video recorder, and everyone is connected to the rest of the world via social media. For Volkswagen to alter its processes and not consider the consequences – both criminally and financially – was nothing short of stupid. It's a sad example of how processes, when ignored or rigged, can come back to bite you and do serious harm to your reputation, job security and bottom line. It's the act of an unconscious company led by inept individuals.

Two concerns companies should have when assessing their work processes are creating complexity and entangling departments that would otherwise function effectively on their own. On the subject of complexity, we think processes should be smooth and easy to follow, not complex. There's no point implementing processes that encumber your people or complicate the manufacturing of your products or service delivery. When reviewing your existing processes, the key is to ask this question: What can we eliminate without compromising the quality of our products or services and further complicating our employees' work? Starting from this vantage point, it will be much easier to streamline your work processes and get buy-in from your people for changes you want to make.

With regard to entangling departments, the key is to have clear boundaries that each department can operate within. While it might be important for the shipping department to work closely with billing and sales, these are three very different functions, and each department's processes must be aligned to enable their respective work teams to operate effectively and smoothly. Too often we experience the opposite. We find support departments such as accounting, payroll, shipping and product development encumbered by processes designed without their input or endorsement from legal, IT and human resources. While these departments manage issues and have company-wide responsibilities, it's important for each department to be in control of their own work processes and their people.

Another common mistake we find is the lack of coordination when a company decides to integrate a new software system. While keeping current with technology is very important, we often see a lack of coordination and communication when it comes to systems integration. Also, the training and retraining of employees on how to fully utilize new systems and software applications to ensure a positive customer experience is paramount to ensuring smooth work processes.

We recently experienced a serious flaw in one client's customer relations management (CRM) system because several employees were working on the same customer files and, as a result, these customers were being contacted three and four times about the same issue by the company's call center. Before the company could fix this glitch, hundreds of customers logged complaints about being harassed by the customer assistance team. The lesson here is get it right the first time, and test and retest it before you experiment on your customers!

The flip side of not updating your work processes to remain competitive should be obvious. One interesting factor we noted in working with a client that had neglected to update its work processes for six years was an attitude of complacency among its employees. These were good people who did the job according to the processes in place. But management never solicited feedback from its employees about how to do their jobs faster, better and smarter. As a result, the employees continued doing the same old thing and they became complacent. It wasn't until competitors started stealing their clients and contracts that management woke up and realized the company's work processes needed to be updated. And who better to ask than the employees who perform the jobs?

We have one final thought regarding processes. It deals with timeliness. Once senior management decides to alter its processes, it's very important to move quickly because those changes can impact productivity, employee morale, customer relationships and your bottom line. Be alert to the fact that sometimes data can be wrong, misinterpreted or inapplicable to your situation. Just because it's factual doesn't mean it's relevant to your situation. Also, data gets stale. We live in a world where things are constantly shifting and changing. What was relevant yesterday might not be as relevant today. We have a favorite expression that goes, "The way it was is not the way it is. And the way it is, is not the way it will be!" Things change, so be sure that your data is fresh, relevant and accurate before you jump in with both feet!

Conscious Business Take-Aways:

1. We recommend you put every policy, procedure and rule on trial for its life at least once every three years. Does your organization really need that policy, rule or procedure? If so, justify it. Obviously, some exist for safety and security while others protect the organization from liability and frivolous lawsuits. Unless your Culture Officer reviews every policy, rule and procedure, you will not know what inhibits employees from doing a better job or creates barriers for your customers to do business with you.

2. How does your work flow? What is the process by which every employee does his/her job? While their processes will differ for each and every job, there should be some continuity and a systematic approach for how work is assigned and gets done. Knowing the answer to this question will save your company time and money. The key is to simplify the process without compromising on safety, reliability and customer satisfaction.

3. When your organization decides to implement a systematic change, are all affected employees brought aboard to help design that change or contribute their two cents as to how that change should work? Oftentimes we find that management arbitrarily decides to change something without ever involving the people who must carry out that change. This is a major mistake on the part of management, and it creates distrust and disengagement among employees.

Chapter 9
The Five Ps of Culture – Performance

The last of our Five Ps is Performance. The ultimate test for every business and organization is its performance. But how do you measure your company's performance? While there are many factors to consider, most companies rely on financial data and metrics to determine their success. We commonly refer to these popular metrics as key performance indicators (KPIs). Among the most popular KPIs are: sales and service revenues, expenses, profit margins, website traffic, inventory, customer loyalty and retention, as well as employee engagement and retention. While KPIs are very important, we find that companies usually only look at KPIs from one dimension – the numbers – while ignoring the other side – that is, the heart and soul of your KPIs. What most companies are missing is viewing their KPIs from a variety of angles and not just the financial perspective.

Here's an example: A few years ago, we spoke at a business conference for financial institutions. One of the speakers, a CFO from a brand name bank, told the attendees that in order to impress upon his bank's employees how well they were being paid, his financial institution was including an annual breakdown of the various benefits paid to employees along with a dollar figure associated with each of these benefits. He referred to this as a Compensation Profile. In each employee's compensation profile, for example, it listed their wages, vacation days, sick leave, health insurance, retirement contribution by the company, and bonus amount. As we sat in the audience listening to him explain his company's rationale for creating and sharing the Compensation Profile with every employee, we noticed a subtle murmuring among the 500 attendees. When the Q&A session began, a woman, who we later learned was a senior vice president at another financial institution, asked the following question: *How was the compensation profile being received by the employees?* The CFO responded that his office had issued four compensation profiles, one every six months for the past two years, and he wasn't aware of any feedback from the employees because the bank had not asked the employees what they thought of it. He added that senior management thought it was a good idea to remind employees that they actually earned much more than just the amount they take home in a pay check.

Interestingly, the woman who asked the question did have some data and she respectfully asked the speaker if she could share her experience on the subject. She told the audience the following. "We tried this once and realized that it was a bad idea because employees resented the suggestion that non-dollar items such as vacation and sick leave were something they were being compensated for when, in fact, it's required by state and federal law." She added, "The conversation around the water cooler in just about every department was negative. Employees felt disrespected and even demoralized by the suggestion that management could somehow put a dollar value on sick leave – but at the same time, discourage employees from using their sick leave to the point where any employee who was sick for more than three days had to provide a written note from their physician!"

"Despite management's best intentions, our employees interpreted the idea as sophomoric and negatively. It's just a bad idea and I would discourage doing it," she concluded. There was polite applause as she sat down. What the woman was telling the audience is that there is a heart-based dimension to performance metrics, and management must be sensitive to balancing their KPIs with heart as well as the numbers. Obviously, the CFO and his bank had never considered the heart side of their Compensation Profile idea. Had they tested it with a focus group of bank employees, they might have learned it was a bad idea that did more harm than good because employees are not robots. They show up and do the best job they can with the tools, resources and direction they receive from management. And when management dangles an inedible carrot such as Compensation Profiles in their face, they resent it. Especially when they can't spend it!

So performance is not just about the numbers side of your business. It's also about how you arrive at those numbers. If management would stop just long enough to understand their employees, they would realize that most companies hire good people who will work hard and go above-and-beyond for the business, provided management pays them fairly, treats them with respect and listens to their ideas. That's it. Again, it's not rocket science, but it does require your C-suite to act with heart and compassion, not just seeing things through dollar signs.

As much as we travel, it never ceases to amaze us when a fellow passenger politely offers a process improvement to a flight attendant. The typical response is this: "Thanks for your suggestion, but management doesn't listen to us and they never ask us for our opinions..." While that may or may not be the case, the perception among many flight attendants we've encountered is management doesn't care what their frontline service champions think. This is pitiful because these are the employees who interact the most with the airline's customers – in other words, the company's largest revenue generators! For a significant percentage of flight attendants to think "management doesn't value our ideas, suggestions or opinions" creates a pirate ship Culture as we noted in the People chapter.

But more importantly, it's demoralizing. Not to pick on the airline industry, but knowing it as well as we do, we realize that there are unions, employee councils and channels for suggestions that every major airline has in place. So the real heart of the issue probably has less to do with "management doesn't listen to us" and more to do with the perception among airline employees that "management treats us like crap! They constantly strip away benefits, change our salary plans, close employee bases, and make us work longer hours for less money!"

Ah-ha! Now we're getting to the heart of the matter. Perhaps the real issue isn't about management not listening to employee suggestions, but rather the underlying issue – and it's true in most organizations that suffer a similar problem – and that problem is management treats us poorly. There's no heart in the C-suite. When this happens, it deflates morale and strips away any incentive on the part of your employees to give you their best performance day-in and day-out. There's an old axiom we encourage senior management to follow: Never discount the message just because you discount the messenger. Good advice is good advice – regardless of the source.

These are just a few reasons why key performance indicators (KPIs) are so important in terms of your corporate Culture. If senior leadership walks its talk and emphasizes its KPIs, many of these problems never surface in the workplace because everyone is reading from the same *Culture Playbook* and striving toward the same goals.

From a Culture standpoint, we believe the following key performance indicators (KPIs) are essential and should be part of every organization's annual Culture Assessment. We have also found that companies, government agencies and non-profit organizations that track these KPIs will likely stay the course to success and profitability.

1. **Revenue from Sales and Service.** Every business and organization must generate revenue to survive and grow. It is the ultimate key performance indicator. Even a government agency generates revenue to sustain its operations. Those agency funds may come from a variety of sources, including Congress, the state legislature, user fees or taxes, but they must generate revenue to function. In the not-for-profit world, revenues come from many sources, including membership dues, conferences, advertising, donations and product sales.

In the for-profit world, revenue comes from sales, service, stocks, warranties, leases and other income streams. The point is, every business lives or dies by its revenue. Most companies closely monitor their revenues on a weekly, monthly and yearly basis to avoid surprises and alter their performance strategies as needed. Every business or organization must generate revenue to sustain itself. Revenue is the lifeblood of your business.

2. **Profit Margin.** Just as every business has revenues, it also has a profit margin. We encourage clients to analyze both their gross profit margin and their net profit margin using the company's leading products or services because this will tell senior management exactly how well or how poorly the company is really performing in the marketplace. While your gross profit margin

reveals your ability to generate sales in a competitive marketplace, your net profit margin is the ultimate key indicator because it tells you the true cost of delivering that product or service to the marketplace. This in turn tells you whether a product or service is sustainable in its present form or should be labeled as a loss-leader.

3. Customer Acquisition. What does it cost you to acquire and maintain customers? As we noted earlier, Dr. Peter Drucker wrote that the "goal of every business is the acquisition and maintenance of its customers." This is why it's important to know how much it cost you to acquire and maintain customers. Most companies arrive at their cost per customer (CPC) by dividing all sales and marketing costs by the number of new clients acquired during a certain period. If, for example, your company spends $50,000 on sales and marketing to acquire 500 new customers, your average CPC is $100. The same calculation works for a specific product or service. If your company spends $100,000 designing, marketing and selling a new widget and you sell 200 widgets, your product cost is $500. So that widget needs to be priced for much more than $500 if you expect to create a healthy profit margin!

4. Customer Retention & Loyalty. The challenge most businesses face is retaining its customers and getting them to spend more money, more often. One reason most major brands have increased their customer care budget is because they know it's significantly cheaper to upsell an existing customer than it is to find a new customer. This is why robotic help desks on the internet, call centers staffed by human beings, and other high-tech, high-touch services are rapidly expanding throughout all sectors of the economy. Nobody wants to lose a customer! It costs too much to replace them.

We like to know from our clients what existing customers spent this year over last year. We also like to know what percentage of customers have returned multiple times or referred family or friends to buy a new car, kitchen appliance, solar panels, or book that fabulous cruise vacation to the Caribbean. This is the cheapest yet most effective marketing you can buy! We refer to these loyal, repeat customers as your Broadcast Customers because they broadcast to the world how wonderful your employees, products and services are. Broadcast Customers are money in the bank! All you have to do is ask your Broadcast Customers for referrals, and perhaps incentivize them with a prize or simple thank you in order to get them to help you expand your business.

5. Website Traffic. The importance of generating website traffic has grown dramatically over the past twenty years since we started tracking key performance indicators related to Culture. Today, your website traffic is among the most important indicators because it tells you many things including: customer demographics, prospective customer demographics, the popularity of your products or services, customer feedback including rants and raves, media coverage, and marketing results based on how well a particular product or service is selling. In a nutshell, if you're not on the web, you're not relevant in today's consumer-based, internet marketing world. You're also leaving money on the table because web-based sales are quickly overtaking brick-and-mortar sales.

6. Employee Engagement & Retention. Just as customer loyalty and retention are essential, so are Employee Engagement & Retention. Two trends that are changing the workplace are (1) revised job descriptions that your employees help craft, and (2) compensation packages that include greater benefits such as healthcare, child leave, sabbaticals and more vacation days. What's somewhat surprising in terms of these trends is that European companies have been very generous when it comes to providing their employees with many of these same benefits, including healthcare and long vacations, whereas American companies have not been as progressive. Now, because there is a talent war where certain skills are highly valued and companies are willing to pay a premium to recruit top performers, the rules have changed. Money and benefits talk! Companies must step up financially or lose talented employees to their competition.

When it comes to re-writing job descriptions, the key is to clearly define what an employee is expected to do, and it matches that particular employee's skills and talents. Most progressive companies are allowing employees to draft their own job descriptions within the boundaries of their departmental needs. This trend has had a very positive impact on higher levels of employee engagement and retention. When you allow employees to tell you what they want to do and how they plan to do it – not to mention fully apply their talents and know-how – they become more vested and kick-it-up a notch in terms of their performance and commitment to the company.

While there are many other KPIs such as Inventory, Backlogs and other financial metrics, these six are the ones we focus on to determine the health of your company's Culture.

Conscious Business Take-Aways:

1. What are your top five key performance indicators (KPIs)? Does every employee know these KPIs and their role in helping their department or organization achieve positive results?

2. Does your company allow its employees to write their own job description so that it reflects their current responsibilities? This is a process that creates significant buy-in among employees and champions performance improvement.

3. Are you using a Culture Assessment to measure your key performance indicators and identify opportunities for improvement? This is one of the most significant values of performing a Culture Assessment. You cannot improve what you don't measure, and you cannot fix what you don't know is broken.

Chapter 10
Culture Role Models: Why Companies Succeed by Leveraging Their Culture

Companies that leverage their Culture all have one thing in common – Success! You'll note that we did not say financial success because that is not the only way to define success in business. While profitability is a significant part of success and a company's overall performance, it's no longer the only key performance indicator. If you are a conscious business or want to become one, you must embrace a much broader definition of success.

While success will be defined differently for each company based on its purpose and principles, a conscious company does not define success only in monetary terms.

We understand and acknowledge that for decades business success was defined in strictly monetary terms. It did not significantly matter how the company managed its operations or whether or not employees were happy, engaged and productive or how much time was focused on customer relationships. If the business generated a profit and consistently stayed in the black, the company was considered successful and management was well-rewarded. But in most companies, it was not the employees.

But times have changed, and so have the expectations of your employees, suppliers, and especially your customers. What is the new definition of success in today's business climate? At CRI Global CAPS, we define success in heartfelt terms. We tell our clients that

153

business is like a coin. It has two distinct and different sides. The first side of the business coin is the financial side. Yes, you must have good financial principles and results in place to achieve success, but there is also another side of the coin. We call it your Culture side because it's all about the heart and soul of your business. When companies take both sides into consideration and focus on balancing them, then and only then will you have a successful business model. Additionally, when both sides of your business coin are balanced, you will have a conscious business.

We are unabashed fans of Sir Richard Branson, who founded the Virgin brand and has guided it masterfully over four decades to success. Today, Virgin has revenues exceeding $20 billion and nearly 80,000 employees. Not every business venture Sir Richard Branson launched was successful. Virgin Cola and Virgin Clothing flopped. But despite setbacks along the way, Branson has always maintained an attitude of "Fail Forward" and he's been unwavering in his passion for people and his commitment to helping every one of his employees achieve a work-life balance, obtain excellent healthcare at a reasonable cost, and earn a livable wage. Today, his daughter Holly, a trained physician, is assuming a more significant leadership role in the company and championing these same causes in order to protect and enhance the Culture at Virgin. When leaders clearly articulate their organization's purpose and goals, and role model the core tenets of its Culture, they are creating a path that any capable person can follow and achieve success. This is the subtle brilliance of Virgin.

During the past ten years, many companies have altered their way of doing business to become a conscious business. Interestingly, while there are many reasons for this transformation, profitability and sustainability are two of the most popular reasons. Yes, that's right! Companies are realizing that in order to be more profitable – and to woo more customers – they need to shift from an unconscious business model to a conscious one.

A conscious company embraces all aspects of its business rather than focusing solely on one specific area, such as generating higher profits. While efficiency measures traditionally dominate the focus for many CEOs, to do so in the current business climate is a mistake and could be a minefield to navigate. Customers are demanding something more from the companies they do business with. To us, this demand is not surprising. We've witnessed the shift firsthand for the past decade. In simple language, customers – especially Millennials and Gen Z'ers – want to do business with companies they feel connected to. It's about heart. If your company makes a profit in the process of connecting with these customers, that's fine by them. But understand the core principle here. It has everything to do with your ability to connect at a heart level. This means your marketing, advertising, customer service, pricing and warranty practices must all be re-examined from the perspective of heart and soul – not profitability. Again, what we have found is rather amazing. Companies like Patagonia, Apple and Amazon that are heart-focused make lots of money and are very profitable! They took the time to figure out how to balance both sides of the coin – profits and people – and become conscious businesses.

This is why Microsoft's Super Bowl LIII television commercial, We All Win, was the most popular ad during the big game. The 2019 commercial featured a nine-year-old handicapped boy from Austin, Texas named Owen Sirmon, who bests an Xbox game and is cheered on by neighborhood kids, led by Owen's close friend, Gunnar Franchione. Owen has Escobar Syndrome, a rare genetic disorder that limits his mobility and makes a wheelchair necessary for long strolls or extended movement. But in the eyes of all those neighborhood kids, Owen isn't limited by his disease. Owen is a winner because he won an Xbox game. That's what all the neighborhood kids see in him – a winner!

At CRI Global CAPS, we help companies focus on the Culture side of the business coin. We give companies a framework and blueprint to assess, define and grow the Culture side of their business coin. We help them connect to the heart of their business with our Five Ps of Culture that we discussed in previous chapters. Companies that elevate their Culture to the prominent place it deserves and leverage their Culture will stand head-and-shoulders above their competition.

Why do you need to leverage your Culture? The answer is simple. There has been a major shift in the global marketplace that emphasizes heart, love and responsibility, and leaders need to adjust their thinking and business practices to this dramatic shift. It's no different than a baseball team shifting its infield players when the opposing batter plans to bunt the ball.

What caused the marketplace shift? The answer is your customers, or more broadly stated, a significant part of society that cares more about people than profits. As more Baby Boomers retire and downsize their households, the new workforce and consumers filling those gaps are Millennials and Gen Z'ers. These new consumers, ages 18-35, have altered how work is done and how products and services are consumed. Every major company knows how this shift is affecting their business in terms of advertising, product design, marketing, sales tactics and pricing. What is ironic is that despite this knowledge, we still find too many companies and government agencies stumbling out of the gate when trying to realign their principles, values and processes with the demands and expectations of a new generation of customers.

Here's the key. Because of this shift, Culture has become a prime focus once again. We are finding too many senior executives who still have their heads stuck in the sand. We've had private conversations with numerous CEOs who told us, "It's just a passing trend; just another generational fad." We respectfully disagree. Our message to every leader in businesses, non-profit organizations and the government sector is this: your Culture needs to align with the wants and needs of a new generation of customers if you want to remain relevant and enjoy a growing market share. Again, we harken back to one of our favorite axioms: *The way it was is not the way it is, and the way it is, is not the way it will be!* Times have changed. The old axiom that "culture trumps strategy every time" has never been more true or relevant.

Any business that believes the old way of thinking ("I have a job for you, take it and like it or leave!") still applies is in serious trouble. While we haven't found any CEOs that embrace this tired, antiquated mantra, we have found too many companies that have not begun their transformation to the *Culture* side of the coin we discussed earlier.

Millennials and Gen Z'ers don't interview for a job hoping you will like them. Instead, they interview you to see if you are a conscious company that they would consider working for. They want to know that the job is tailored to their talents and ambitions, that the position you've advertised will fulfill their needs as much as supplying them with a reasonable paycheck. And here's the catch. If your company isn't able or willing to meet their expectations, they'll go to work for your competition! That's the reality we currently live in. It's very much an employee's market, not an employer's market. Whether you're hiring people to work in your fast food restaurant or hiring an engineer to help you advance sustainability, good talent is hard to find, and great talent is even harder to recruit because Culture matters to these candidates.

If you're in senior management, ask yourself these questions: Why would your company allow your best-and-brightest employees and/or recruits to slip away and go to work for your competition? Is it simply a question of paying them a few thousand dollars more to keep them or is it a question of expanding your vacation or leave policy? Or, perhaps, is it a question of providing better healthcare benefits?

We interviewed one vice president of human resources for a major Fortune 500 company who told us his company lost over 20 highly-talented software engineers to a competitor because his CFO was unwilling to match a signing bonus of $25,000 per employee that was being offered by the competition, which had recently relocated to their headquarters city. The vice president of human resources shook his head in disbelief as he told us the cost of replacing all that talent far exceeded $25,000 for each new hire. Once again, when the bean counter mentality is running your business and making narrow-minded decisions based solely on dollars and cents, poor judgment will prevail and bad decisions will be made.

Along with the shifting demands of employees, the demands of consumers have changed as well. We now live in a world of instant gratification. Products and services not only need to be delivered quickly, but doing business with your company must give consumers a good feeling. No one wants to do business with a company that has a poor reputation or suffers from arrogance. Your reputation in the marketplace can make or break your company. Having a positive and *balanced Culture* will manage and eliminate reputational risk.

We are finding that more companies are focusing on Culture as a way to add heart into their business model, as well as managing risk. They want to balance the business coin. We have found that a company that leads with heart and focuses on its purpose, principles, people, processes and performance will achieve marketplace success and profitability.

It's important to re-emphasize that your processes – including financial efficiency – are very important to a company's success. Obviously, you need to monitor the impact of major expenditures to your business, but when the red pencil is all that is used to create a profit, you will have failed to leverage your Culture. That will most assuredly result in an unbalanced, unconscious business model. The result will be customer defection and, eventually, less revenue.

How does a company leverage their Culture to enhance their bottom line? Let's look at an actual case study to demonstrate how a business went from being an unconscious business to a conscious business, and ultimately improved its bottom line. The company name and industry has been changed but the facts remain the same.

The Case of the Water Widgets (WW) Company

WW manufactures water meter parts and has performed very well over the past six decades. Established in 1952, the company has steadily improved its bottom line every year with only two exceptions. Both downturns occurred during recessions. The first was 1974-1975, the second was 2008-2010. On average, WW's assets grew by 18-20% annually for the past ten years. As WW has grown, they added staff and new product lines to keep current in the marketplace. WW has also continued to upgrade its systems and technologies.

WW has contracts with over 150 municipalities across the country to supply water meter parts for both older and newer meters. In recent years, two other companies have entered the water meter market and for the first time, WW is facing serious competition.

In a six-month period, WW lost three major contracts worth millions of dollars. Management was very concerned and held a series of meetings to discuss how to reverse this negative trend. No major course corrections had been determined or implemented because they were not sure what to do. WW asked us to help them leverage their Culture to stay competitive in their market.

The first thing we suggested to WW was to conduct a Culture Assessment to find out where they placed on the *Culture Spectrum*™. The Culture Assessment would help them determine where deficiencies existed and, based on this knowledge, we could then create a *Culture Playbook* to address their deficiencies.

We believed that the answers and directions they were seeking were contained within the parameters of the Five Ps of Culture. We advised WW not to reduce staff, limit employee benefits or eliminate employee appreciation events until their Culture Assessment was completed. We've learned from experience that making efficiency corrections as a knee-jerk response to declining income was premature and often unnecessary in the final analysis.

What did WW find after conducting their Culture Assessment? WW found that they had fallen into the Under-Performing category on our *Culture Spectrum*™. Taking a closer look at their assessment results, we examined each aspect of the Five Ps of Culture.

Purpose. We found that WW's purpose was still valid. The company was created in 1952 to "manufacture and supply reliable water meter parts for our valued customers." Today, their products and services remain vital to hundreds of municipalities across the United States, and the market remains active as the demand for new, technologically-smart water meter parts grows. We also found that their existing product line – including the servicing of their water meter parts – was competitive and adequate.

Principles. We found that WW's principles and values had not changed, been ignored or compromised while conducting their business over the past decade. No corners were cut, nor did they fail to maintain the standards they set for themselves over 60 years prior. WW set out to be a leader in their field and they have continued in that direction. We did find that WW needed to update their Mission Statement so it accurately reflected the global aspects of their business and the reality of new competitors.

Processes. Looking at many processes, we found a major issue with WW's marketing and sales processes. At CRI Global CAPS, we consider marketing and sales to be two of the most important processes when it comes to manufacturing. While quality and safety are also essential, much of the misalignment within WW's processes were found in the two critical areas of sales and marketing. This deficiency was contributing to their loss of business.

When WW was the only major supplier of water meter parts, their sales and marketing initiatives were not as critical. Customers came to them because they were the most reputable company manufacturing these parts. But when the competition showed up and the competition started demonstrating the superior quality of their products and services, WW did not respond. They failed to make changes to their sales and marketing processes to account for the new competition. WW failed to step into the ring and fight. They failed to become competitive. They did not advertise in trade magazines nor did they update their website. They failed to schedule their salesforce to meet with existing customers and ask for leads or new client referrals. In other words, they failed to build long-term customer relationships. When we interviewed former clients, we heard two common themes – "We never hear from WW" and "They took our business for granted."

We recommended a sales and marketing meeting at which everyone involved in these two areas – including their support staff and related functions – gather for two days to talk about the changes that were needed, and to let the brilliance of their employees shine by providing solutions to meet the new competition head-on.

After facilitating a successful off-site meeting, a dynamic new sales and marketing strategy emerged with actionable steps and clearly defined goals. Accountability for maintaining existing clients and finding new customers was a major part of this new strategy.

People. In every organization, your goldmine is your people. Their brilliance and innovative spirit is limitless. Gone are the days when job descriptions are merely a list of duties. We coach our clients to add Core Power descriptions as well. While we describe Core Powers in more detail in Chapter 13, Core Powers help individuals use their intuitive and technical brilliance. While specific skills may be required to perform certain jobs, such as an engineer or physician, it is the Core Power within each person that drives their brilliance and helps them utilize their unique skills.

For WW, we had to be sure that the members of the marketing and sales team understood their Core Powers and how to use them in light of WW's new sales and marketing strategy, as well as corporate expectations. Sales teams that are trained to use their Core Powers will always better relate and connect to their customers' needs.

Performance. WW spent considerable time examining the Performance dimension of their *Culture Spectrum*™. The manufacturing process needed some streamlining, but overall it worked fine. Some equipment used in the process of manufacturing water meter parts was old and this slowed production and hurt them in terms of competing with companies that could deliver similar parts faster. Several new pieces of equipment were purchased to increase WW's manufacturing capabilities and expedite product delivery across most of their top revenue-generating product lines. While there was a sizeable investment, the savings would be recovered within two years by attracting more clients who had an immediate need for water meter parts, especially after floods, hurricanes and other natural disasters had damaged those municipalities' water systems.

Next, WW had all their employees complete our Core Power Assessment™ as a way of improving job satisfaction across the company. The results were impressive, and the employee feedback from this assessment revealed that employees felt more connected to their jobs and each other. Also, by completing the Core Power Assessment™, employees from various departments started communicating with each other for the first time in years. No longer were accounting and procurement isolated from sales or senior management. The human resources department at WW deserved kudos for the work they did in helping employees revise their job descriptions and duties with their Core Powers. It was very much a discovery process for many long-term employees at WW who never knew they possessed certain talents and abilities that heretofore were undiscovered and went unnoticed and unused in the company. Interestingly, it cost WW nothing to tap into this deep reservoir of newfound talent.

The outcome of the Culture Assessment was felt immediately by the company. Longtime clients renewed contracts as sales and marketing efforts took on a new focus and intensity to build and maintain customer relationships. Client satisfaction improved, and new competitive pricing models attracted more customers as a direct result of WW updating its production methods.

Once WW got serious and leveraged its Culture to create a plan to turn their business around, it also added heart to balance the bottom line. Two years later, WW was back in the black and winning more business because it operated as a conscious business using the principles and tools from *The Heart and Soul of Culture*.

Conscious Business Take-Aways

1. It's important for leadership to listen. We know that no one has all the answers, but the answers are there if you learn to listen to enough people and ask your key stakeholders what they think.

2. To become a successful conscious business, you must balance both sides of your business coin. Business requires a focus on both financial and cultural aspects. Is your business focused on both financial and Culture aspects?

3. When was the last time you conducted a Culture audit to assess your Culture performance and learn how to leverage your Culture for business success?

Chapter 11
The Culture Phenomena:
Why Customers Love a Winner!

There's no doubt about it – a winning spirit is good for business! If you watch any sporting competition, you know how much people enjoy cheering for their team and experiencing the feelings of elation that comes with winning. In professional sports, a winning season usually ensures greater ticket sales for the team the following season. Winning an Olympic medal opens many endorsements and other enriching opportunities for the victorious athletes. Whether or not you're a fan of the National Football League's New England Patriots, you have to admire and respect the fact that this talented team has played in 11 Super Bowls and won six of those championship games!

Winning, at its most basic level, is all about survival. In prehistoric days, a caveman was considered victorious if he made it through the day and was still alive by nightfall. While times have changed, the thrill of victory and celebrating a winner remains among the most basic human instincts.

This sentiment is true in business as well. One of the easiest ways to attract and keep customers is to provide a winning solution for your customers or to be recognized as a best-in-class company.

A business cannot succeed without customers. In business, to be a winner you need to have customers that celebrate you, champion your products, and choose your products and services over those of your competition. You also want your loyal customers to sing your praises across social media. At CRI Global CAPS we call these people *Broadcast Customers*. The key reason they extol your virtues so loudly is because they identify with your brand and feel like they're doing business with a winner!

Winning companies that know how to leverage Culture rarely have to worry about losing money or damaging their reputation. In fact, companies who are Culture winners often enjoy a constant and steady flow of Broadcast Customers. Attracting or retaining them is done consciously; it's part of their Culture. Winning companies don't struggle to maintain their bottom line. Yes, they work at it, just like every other business does, but because these companies champion a Culture of winning, they know what it takes to win, and they win more often. That's the Culture of a winner – they win!

Winning in business requires two key factors. First and foremost, we believe you must have a balanced work Culture. Second, you must use efficiency measures that protect your bottom line while developing the full potential of your employees, customers or suppliers. As the legendary NBA basketball coach Pat Riley once said, "It may be simple, but it isn't easy!" Creating a winning Culture really boils down to understanding your numbers and managing your Culture. Interestingly, it was NBA coach Pat Riley who developed a winning Culture with the Los Angeles Lakers by focusing on free-throws. Coach Riley understood that if his basketball team could sink just two more free-throw shots per game at the foul line, the odds changed dramatically in terms of a win versus a loss.

At CRI Global CAPS, we have found that a company that fails to balance this delicate business coin – profits and people – by creating a balanced approach to the numbers and preserving its Culture, risks becoming an unconscious business. Unconscious businesses are rarely winners, and as we've previously noted, most pirate ships are eventually sunk!

When a business places equal importance to their efficiency methods while protecting its Culture, they become a conscious business and eventually, a winner. Customers love to do business with companies that are proven winners. It makes them feel good. We realize that what we're talking about here is typically classified by organizational development experts as intangibles, but the reality is that a customer's feelings and emotions are largely responsible for their buying decisions. Feelings matter. Being excited about a winning team matters! It spurs people to take action, to cheer, to buy more team memorabilia and attend more games. In the case of a company's Culture, we define feelings as the employees' and customers' perceptions of the overall energy of a particular business. With transparent methods for measuring customer and employee perception such as Yelp and Glassdoor, it's not hard to see in black and white terms what the energy level of any business is.

Read through most of the reviews on these two popular websites and you will better understand how customers, employees and suppliers really feel about a company. Yelp reviews are often focused on a business's service performance, while Glassdoor provides some unique insights as to how a company treats its employees. No longer can you hide your dirty laundry or sweep your corporate problems under the proverbial rug. Everything is out there in plain view for the world to see. As one CEO told us, "We live in an era where everybody has a camera. Everything I do is visible. I cannot afford to say something stupid or insensitive because I cannot take it back, ever!" Consider John Schnatter of Papa John's Pizza, who uttered some very insensitive and damaging words that went viral. It seriously hurt his reputation and tarnished not only his name, but the brand of Papa John's Pizza.

Companies that are winners make their customers feel good about their products and services as well as the way they do business. How else do you explain the success of Starbucks? Yes, Starbucks coffee tastes good, but at an average price of over $3.50 per cup, is it that much better than a .99 cent cup of coffee from McDonald's or Dunkin Donuts? The answer according to any Starbucks customer is a resounding *Yes*!

The priorities for what a customer desires determines who they choose to do business with. Once a customer chooses a company they want to do business with, it is up to the company to make the customer feel like they are doing business with a winner.

For customers of Patagonia, Cotopaxi and REI, three excellent outdoor gear companies, it's about quality and comfort while braving the elements. These companies are winners in their industry. If you want a variety of products and you want them delivered fast and at a competitive price, you choose Amazon because they deliver just that! That's what makes Amazon a winner. Apple gives you technology that is innovative, functional and beautiful. That is their winning strategy. Hopefully you get the idea. Whether you are a fan of these companies or not, they offer winning solutions to their customers and that's why they have so many Broadcast Customers and rave reviews on social media sites.

Companies that are winners employ people who don't embarrass them. They don't consciously cut corners in any way that compromises the company's reputation, and they manage their bottom lines and Cultures to make sure they perform like winners. This is how they attract top employees and high-spending customers. They know how to manage their Cultures by having and using a *Culture Playbook*.

As a business, you can't let down your guard for one minute. This is what happened to Facebook, another good company, but one that allowed a broken process and bad policy that was counter to its reputational Culture to go unchecked. Facebook's leadership committed a serious and costly blunder by letting its user data be pirated by unscrupulous third parties. You always need to be focused on how you are perceived in the world. When you have a *Culture Playbook*, you have a system in place and a framework for always making sure you are doing the right thing in accordance with your Mission, Values and Principles. This ensures your company will always be on the winning side of business. Facebook forgot this lesson and it cost them dearly.

People love winners because winning teams and organizations make us feel like winners! When the French soccer team won the 2018 FIFA World Cup, jubilant fans around the world celebrated the team's success. Celebrants weren't limited to French citizens waving flags. Millions of soccer fans cheered the French team for its victory. Why? Because everyone loves a winner, and everyone wants to identify with a winner.

But when a winner starts to lose, many once-faithful fans and customers flee. Sometimes as a leader, you will find yourself standing alone when you hit a losing streak. If you've ever stood at a craps table in Las Vegas when a gambler is hot and winning, there is always a crowd watching his or her every roll of the dice. The crowd around the table shares in the excitement as the pile of chips grows higher. Roll after roll, the crowd and excitement builds, leading to cheering, high-fives and rooting for more good luck to appear despite the house odds.

But what happens when lady luck runs out and the gambler's hot streak ends? The crowd thins out and leaves in search of the next winner. The same thing happens in business. We have outlined actual stories for you to show what happens when there is a breakdown in Culture. In most cases, we can clearly see what went wrong and what factors caused a company's winning streak to end. As authors and consultants, we get the benefit of our hindsight being 20/20 and being Monday morning quarterbacks.

Early in our consulting career we were told by a very wise CEO that risk was all about managing perception. Your reputation has a priceless price tag. He was so right. At CRI Global CAPS, we don't let our clients forget that winning and reputational leadership go hand-in-hand. The challenge in managing risk is always keeping an eye on what is going on in all aspects of your business. Culture shifts, and if you're not paying attention, risk can increase. That's why we strongly advocate for creating a *Culture Playbook* to managing your company's Culture and limit your risks. You can't win if you don't know how to play the game. Beginner's luck is short-lived. The challenge is to remain in the game and play it well. Again, we encourage you to study winners and examine why they consistently win. What are they doing right that you can emulate?

For many companies, the proactive focus has always been on the numbers and quarterly earnings report. These companies feel that the majority of the company's risk is managed solely by focusing on its success as told only by the numbers. The Culture aspect of many companies is an afterthought and is only focused on by necessity, usually after something negative has happened. It's akin to closing the barn door after the horse runs away. This was Facebook's big problem – convincing users that their data was safe.

We've also noticed that companies driven solely by the numbers often delegate the management of Culture and risk management to Human Resources or its legal department. Many CEO's believe that managing the expectations of employees is the only Culture issue that needs to be managed. We hear from many

HR departments that it's their job to make their employees happy – to do whatever it takes as long as it doesn't cost much money. This approach is a classic Culture mistake. It is also a classic failure when it comes to managing the entire Culture spectrum. HR should not be in charge of managing the full spectrum of a company's Culture. It's not a job they are trained to do. Culture cannot be considered a necessary burden and, therefore, dumped in the lap of human resource experts or any other department that is not trained to handle it.

If you have not caught on by now, we think that Culture is more visible than money when it comes to attracting new customers and keeping existing ones. Culture is about showing your best face, doing the right thing, and honestly communicating with customers about your products and services. When you think about Apple, for instance, you probably picture beautiful and useful products, cutting edge innovation, futuristic thinking, and music before you ever think about how much money those products cost or how much revenue they generate. There is no hidden agenda. What you see is what you get. Apple doesn't pretend to be anything other than what they stand for. And their products are not the cheapest on the market. In fact, Apple products are usually at the higher end of the technology spectrum when it comes to iPhones and computers. Just like Starbucks, customers tend to flock to Apple because they love their products, service and what the company stands for. Winners attract winners!

The worst thing a company can do is to portray a phony Culture. In other words, they pretend to care about their customers and appear to offer products or services that are customer-friendly, but on the back side, the opposite is true. Everything they do is focused on making money. Then they cover up their real intentions by creating a false persona through fake marketing. For example, not honoring warranties or coupons, or using bait n' switch tactics that are not only morally wrong, but also illegal. This is usually done by unconscious businesses run by profit-driven management. Rarely have we found cases where senior management has not known what's going on. After all, that's their job – to be in the know! In the case of Wells Fargo Bank, when CEO John Stumpf testified before the United States Congress, he said he was unaware of his bank's fake-account practices – in which 5,300 employees secretly created millions of unauthorized bank and credit card accounts without their customers knowing it – the bank's board of directors was so embarrassed by Stumpf's public remarks and lack of awareness as to what was happening inside his own bank that they were forced to fire him.

At the other end of the spectrum, there are times when a company implements a new process or launches a new product that it creates unforeseen problems in other departments. Our research reveals that most of these problems or backlash situations are the result of poor communication within the organization's hierarchy and the unconscious practice of management not involving every department that could possibly be affected in the product's pre-launch planning phase. What we're talking about here is not rocket science, it's really common sense and prudent management practices!

When we analyzed the Volkswagen emissions control cheating scandal a few years ago, it was obvious that there was a blatant cover-up perpetrated at multiple levels of the company. This Culture breach of VW's ethics created false truths, lies and a very costly scandal that resulted in a reputational loss of leadership, lawsuits, the firing of senior executives and the felony conviction of employees who engaged in fraud and misrepresentation.

When you see a company in trouble, it's often caused by flaws in their approach to Culture. Typically, one or more of The Five Ps has fallen gravely out of balance and the troubled company doesn't have a *Culture Playbook* to either alert them to the problem or properly manage the risk. In the case of Facebook, here is an example of an excellent company that fell from grace. While the business took a financial hit, it was its reputational leadership position and respect in the social media world that took the biggest hit. Thousands of customers closed their Facebook accounts because Facebook lost their trust on many levels. A healthy Culture manages risk day-in and day-out. So what happened at Facebook?

From a Culture perspective, it appears that Facebook founder, Mark Zuckerberg, admitted to losing control of his Culture. His people, including Facebook's Chief Operating Officer, Sheryl Sandberg, neglected to apply the most important P to the growing business model. That P is Principle. The most important principle Facebook must honor is to keep customer data safe at all costs. It seems that Facebook put money and profits ahead of protecting its users' data. If this is true, one could make the case that the "profit paradigm" caused Facebook to turn a blind eye to one of its sacred principles, and now they are paying a steep price for their negligence. Ironically, Sandberg, who worked at Google before joining Facebook, has been quoted as saying, "Done is better than perfect." Perhaps it was this philosophy that led to Facebook's troubles. When it comes to protecting users' data, you cannot afford to settle for anything less than perfect.

Did Facebook succumb to greed by allowing paying advertisers to become more important than data safety? In defense of Facebook, the company has strongly denied that the leak of Facebook user data to Cambridge Analytica was connected in any way to Facebook's advertising business. That statement would appear to be both true and rational since software developers did not fall under Sandberg's area of responsibility. But Sandberg has defended the business practice that relies on the mass collection of Facebook users' data, telling the media that "it benefits consumers." But when a significant number of Facebook users deleted their accounts or reduced the time they spent on Facebook because of the improper harvesting of their data, it's apparent that Facebook's senior management was wrong.

While Zuckerberg hired and entrusted Sheryl Sandberg to set policies and manage the overall activities of his highly successful social media company, her lack of vigilance over the security of data and user privacy is very troubling to us because obviously the most important policies (data safety and privacy) never got set or implemented. As capable as Sandberg has been in managing Facebook's business success, it appears there was a major gap in Facebook's Culture blueprint – no one in Facebook's senior ranks thought to ask the all-important question, "If we allow a company like Cambridge Analytica, or the other 60 preferred vendors, to access our user data via a personality quiz (which 300,000 Facebook users downloaded in 2014), what could go wrong? The answer, of course, is "Everything!" It all hit the fan!

When one of your core tenets or principles is undermined, your company can quickly become a loser instead of a winner. This is what's happening to Facebook. They failed to adhere to their core tenets. As the business expanded and new products and services were added, privacy principles became diluted. As new employees were hired and new divisions were created to accommodate Facebook's explosive growth, we think Facebook's core principles – relating to its Culture – got lost in the mix. This is a cardinal sin and it falls squarely on the shoulders of senior management.

Have you ever played the old game of telephone? The first person whispers a sentence such as, "Have you ever played with a basket of puppies?" This same question gets whispered down the line. When it gets to the last person, the sentence has been grossly misinterpreted and translated. It's always different at the end than when it started. Typically, the last person in the whispering chain ends up with a sentence such as, "Putting together a basket of poppies is fun." It's very interesting to analyze what happened and why. How could such a simple sentence become so distorted? Unfortunately, this is exactly what happens in many businesses.

If you ever watched the graphic war movie, Tora! Tora! Tora! the dramatic retelling of the Pearl Harbor attack on December 7, 1941, there were a series of obvious signs that, if recognized, signaled the eminent attack by Japan's Imperial Navy on U.S. Forces at Pearl Harbor, but nobody in the U.S. Navy or Army's senior command put two-and-two together. By the time a Navy commander in Washington, D.C. figured out that Japan was going to attack Pearl Harbor, it was too late, and the results were devastating for American forces in Hawaii. As a result, the United States was drawn into World War II.

Oftentimes we see the same thing happening in business. Well-defined processes, when they start out, often end up changed as a result of massive growth and the profit paradigm. The resulting processes end up violating principles and processes that should be cherished and not changed. Or if they need to be revamped, leadership must ensure the necessary oversight takes place to protect the integrity of its core principles and virtues as it alters its processes to remain competitive and relative to its customers. If you don't see conflicting processes, you are building your business on a shaky foundation. If you want to remain a winner, don't build a house of cards.

This is the "Facebook Syndrome" as we refer to it. An excellent young company has a Culture that appears to be built out of a house of cards. New processes undermined their most important principal – keeping user data safe. It's hard to explain how such competent leadership couldn't notice that one flawed process could cause such a violation of data security. Perhaps they underestimated to what lengths the "data pirates" would go to abuse their data. Certainly there was an operational failure when there was no monitoring of the actions of the people they were sharing data with, especially one led by a political operative. While we don't fault Facebook for this data piracy abuse, we feel it is clearly the error of the company's senior management when people don't see the potential for this kind of data theft and abuse when management was responsible for creating the conflicting process in the first place. Feeling that contractual protection was enough, it was at best a weak and ineffective option. Communication breakdowns most certainly played a part as well.

As we go to print, there is another disturbing issue we see within Facebook. That is, does Facebook really need to care about data piracy and data abuse by app developers? We raise this question because Facebook is the proverbial 800-pound gorilla in terms of social media and online networking, and it's certainly the best at what it does. Millions of new users are flocking to the social media giant regardless of its past miscues and data abuses.

Despite the fact that Zuckerberg told Congress that his company is a "technology company," we would define Facebook as an American online social media and social networking service company. Regardless of how one classifies the company, Facebook remains the most popular social media and networking businesses in the free world. We think this fact creates a serious dilemma and moral challenge for Facebook. As the world's most popular online social media and networking service, can it make its own rules regarding the sharing of user data and the security of that user data? Given its huge market value and net worth, Facebook certainly can afford to pay fines and penalties for legal violations, data breaches and data piracy.

Equally important, with so many new users signing up by the thousands every day, Facebook continues to dominate the online social media and network marketplace. So does it need to worry about broken processes or user complaints? Maybe not. Frankly, that concerns us because any company that is that powerful and operates outside the boundaries of a moral code is dangerous.

Hopefully, Zuckerberg and Sandberg have sharpened their focus on Facebook's Culture and will revive their company's tarnished reputation while honoring their core principles. We hope they will look at all their processes with a heightened sense of urgency and examine all the pieces to eliminate any loop holes, black holes and mud holes that could derail them in the future. It's a painful lesson for any company to learn, but hopefully one Facebook can build on and will continue to advance the twin pillars of social media and data security.

If we were giving them advice on how to recover, we would tell them to become the shining example of how a company comes together to build a process to audit every layer of its operation and employee awareness to make data safety Priority One. They must also be truthful and honest at all levels to get to the bottom of this problem. You cannot cover up a mistake of this magnitude. Too many people know the truth, so let it out. To become winners again, Facebook must be transparent about how they solve their user data problem and build a stronger foundation based on the Five Ps of Culture. They also need to create a *Culture Playbook* if they haven't done so already.

As users of Facebook's services, we like what they do, but we are also aware of how hard it is to guard their users' data while continuing to increase their bottom line. Hopefully Facebook will set new standards for data safety and data piracy protection, and raise the bar for every social media company when it comes to safeguarding their customers' data.

If you are a CEO who defines winning only by the profit paradigm, you should know you are building your own house of cards. How do you shore up your processes and principles? We have discovered that those companies that leverage their Culture by creating and abiding by their *Culture Playbook* are the winners that customers love.

Conscious Business Take-Aways:

1. Does your organization have a winning game plan? Have you engaged your key stakeholders in the process of designing your service delivery and brand protection program?
2. Are you prepared for a crisis? Does your company have a rapid response team in place to handle internal miscues as well as natural disasters that impact employees and customers?
3. Do your leaders have the courage to face the music when things go wrong? Is senior leadership willing to step forward and be held accountable for its decisions and actions? This is part of a leader's role.

Chapter 12
Conscious Business Tools to Transform Your Business

Long before we started writing *The Heart and Soul of Culture*, we were determined to provide our readers with tools to raise the level of consciousness to survive and thrive in the often fickle and changing business economy. We knew a list of conscious business tools was necessary in order to provide our readers with the focus and direction to get there.

Before we share several essential conscious business tools with you, it might be helpful to address exactly what we mean by a Conscious Business.

Conscious Capitalism is a global movement co-founded by John Mackey, CEO of Whole Foods Market, and Raj Sisodia, Ph.D., a renowned author and business leader.

According to the Conscious Capitalism movement, this business philosophy builds on the foundations of Capitalism – voluntary exchange, entrepreneurship, competition, and free trade. While most recognize that these are essential to a healthy economy, Conscious Capitalism also includes the critical elements of trust, compassion and collaboration. Companies like Trader Joe's, Costco, Panera and Southwest Airlines have adopted this business approach as a way of thinking about capitalism and business to embrace the human journey, the state of our world, and the innate potential of business to make a positive impact on the world.

The Conscious Capitalism movement also challenges business leaders to re-think why their organizations exist and to acknowledge their companies' roles in the interdependent global marketplace. As part of this new approach to achieving higher profits, Conscious Capitalism promotes four tenets: Higher Purpose, Stakeholder Integration, A Conscious Culture, and Conscious Leadership.

We're particularly intrigued by the Conscious Culture tenet that encourages companies to embody values, principles and practices that underlie the social fabric of a business which, in turn, permeate its actions and connects the stakeholders to each other and to the company's purpose, people and processes.

A Conscious Culture also fosters love and care and builds trust between a company's team members and its other stakeholders. Conscious Culture is an energizing and unifying force that truly brings a Conscious Business to life.

Here is a beginning list of conscious business tools we think every business should consider.

Assessments:

Assessments offer valuable information and perspective to a business. How do you know you are moving in the right direction if you don't ask key questions of your customers, employees and suppliers?

Customer Assessments provide you with a clear picture in terms of knowing that what you're doing is working. Our companies who routinely ask customers about existing business processes often find great relief in knowing that what they are doing makes sense to their customers. Keeping customers happy and referring new business is good for your business. Likewise, if an assessment tells them what they are doing is not working, a course correction is far better than managing a disaster.

We have companies that assess a wide variety of processes, and while you hope the information returned is helpful and positive, it can be even more useful if it comes back with negative results. Either way, you have a clear picture of what you need to focus on and possibly improve.

Business Partners and Supplier Assessments: We have clients that send assessments to business partners and suppliers. Our clients tell us that many business enhancements have come from asking a list of simple questions to the people who help them do business. Oftentimes, a new and better way of doing business has emerged, especially as technology continues to change. One client improved their shipping process dramatically, leading to a higher customer satisfaction response. Our client had no idea the new process was available to them until they asked. What does that tell you? If you don't ask, you don't get!

Employee Assessments are important, and at CRI Global CAPS we feel it should be an annual process. We have clients who ask their employees to evaluate the company's performance every year. This is just a smart business practice. Employee assessments help to keep employees engaged and happy. Happy employees are like Broadcast Customers. They invite their friends to come and work with them which lessens the recruiting and hiring nightmare many companies face.

A few years ago we had a client ask their employees a simple question. "If you could suggest one new product or service that we could offer our customers, what would it be?" The ideas poured in, but one idea made so much sense because it was simple, and when it was launched, it boosted the bottom line and created opportunities for greater creativity in the division. Yes, one simple question created new revenue of over two million dollars in the first year! What was the idea, you ask? A special pre-sale invitation by email to their preferred customers that offered a 10% discount coupon if they purchased on a certain day before the sale and did so online.

Never underestimate the power and profitability of an assessment!

Culture Playbook:

A *Culture Playbook* is a Conscious Business Tool. In the next chapter we outline for you the importance of developing and using a *Culture Playbook*. As a tool for measuring reputational risk, there is nothing better.

A key point worth noting is the benefit a *Culture Playbook* offers to a company's CEO and senior leadership.

Interestingly, we find that CEOs are often the last people to know if the company Culture is starting to slip below the water line. CEOs are often focused in so many directions that it's hard to look at the overall picture when it comes to examining the Five Ps side of the coin.

When a CEO mandates the creation of a *Culture Playbook*, it ensures that someone will be watching out for the company's best interests and alerting her/him to any potential reputational icebergs in its path. A *Culture Playbook* is also an excellent tool for proactively monitoring any operational or financial consequences resulting from business or economic changes. A well-crafted *Culture Playbook* creates a very high-level set of eyes in one comprehensive document.

A *Culture Playbook* can be a CEO's best time/risk management tool.

Core Power System™:

The Core Power System™ will raise the conscious aspect of your business exponentially because it raises the energy and feelings of satisfaction of your employees. This may be a bold statement but we have found it to be true with every client we have worked with.

Each of us possesses eight fundamental core powers. It is the arrangement of an individual's Core Powers that make us uniquely different from one another. The beauty of the Core Power System™ is that if you know yourself, you know everyone else. This is important because it enhances understanding and communication within the ranks.

Unlike other assessment tools you may have previously used, you have a very short list of common traits to understand. When we understand our co-workers, that understanding builds and enhances performance across an organization.

Enhancing knowledge of our core powers helps us choose how we do things at a very fundamental level. When we work with a client to assess the core powers of their employees, we find the employees delight in understanding how they show up. It may come as a surprise to an employee, but many people already have some knowledge of their Core Powers.

The bottom line benefit to an organization is in the preparation of performance evaluations. As a manager, you understand what it takes to create an employee evaluation that is meaningful and constructive. Enter the Core Power System™ and that struggle is behind you.

At CRI Global CAPS, we encourage our clients to look at their employee evaluations from two perspectives. The first perspective is job specific competencies. Are they performing the job duties outlined in the job description? That's the easy part since it's a yes or no question.

The second part of the evaluation focuses on the employee's Core Powers and how they are applying their core powers to their job requirements. When an employee understands and leverages their Core Powers in the performance of their job, the satisfaction and engagement of the employee is limitless. Both the manager and employee have an opportunity to suggest more ways of merging his/her Core Powers with the job requirements.

Several years ago, we had a client who came to us with an employee retention problem. They advised us that the staff seemed lackluster and tired. The side effect of the lack of engagement was that sick days had increased and, for the first time, our client noticed employees were quitting at a higher rate than usual.

As the first step, we created an assessment focused on engagement and satisfaction. An alarming 68% of the responses from the employees said they didn't feel connected to the company's mission and couldn't see how they made a difference in the work they were performing. We also found that the employees said they were not sure they were adequately performing their work in light of some recent changes made to company structure and positions. In short, everyone felt lost, including several members of the management team.

We immediately suggested that the employees be given a core power assessment and group training on how to use the assessment to reconnect to their work. The assessment process took two weeks and the group training was done in three sessions to meet the scheduling needs of the employees.

The results were exciting! Most people connect to their assessment results. They like to see their Core Powers in a black and white format and when they do, they feel a tangible connection to their Core Powers that extends far beyond an occasional, fleeting connection. The curve on most results show there are some people who fully understand how they are wired. Likewise, on the bottom end, there are people who just can't see their Core Powers. The bulk of the people fall in between the top and bottom groups and benefit tremendously from the clear understanding and interpretation of their Core Powers.

We sometimes advise our clients to offer two additional training sessions focusing on the top and bottom groups. One training session is custom-designed for those fully engaged employees to get them quickly focused on how to integrate their Core Powers into their job. This group is comprised of those employees you don't want to lose to your competition. Giving them the chance to further define their job capabilities in a way that is authentic is very valuable to them.

At the other end of the spectrum, we host a training session for those employees who are disengaged. Obviously, we never label these employees as such, but everyone knows who they are. Oftentimes we find this group needs to be coached to understand their Core Powers, and once they understand, they need to be nurtured and encouraged to apply them on the job.

We find in this group that they are more connected with a core power farther down the list of eight rather than in their top two. Once we open the door to the reality of what they have at their disposal they perk-up. Missing the obvious is often the result of beliefs they have about themselves that are just not true. Clearing up their personal misconceptions helps tremendously. Some gentle coaching creates new beliefs when backed with events from past life experiences that clearly demonstrate that they had the Core Powers all along.

One example we can share with you involved an employee named Bill. Bill was a manager in a company that imported and distributed flowers throughout the United States. Bill was a wonderful manager of people and he thought his staff loved him, but the fact was that Bill was not well-liked by many of his employees because he was gruff and too blunt. Despite having a good heart, Bill's bluntness often created a negative impression among his employees and suppliers. He was perceived as overbearing at times. People would see Bill coming and try to avoid him.

It was not surprising that Bill's primary Core Power was that of a "Truth Teller." Truth Tellers will tell you how it is, straight and to the point. They can also be bullies because they insist on being right. Bill acknowledged that he did give off the impression of needing to be right, especially if frustrated. The secret to being a successful Truth Teller is knowing how and when to share your truth.

To balance things out, we told Bill his secondary Core Power was that of the "Communicator." Communicators love words and teaching. There is nothing they cannot explain. Secretly, Communicators want to hide away and write a book. We explained to Bill that when telling the truth, he should try to make it a learning experience for his team, not a parent-child scolding. Explain why something should be happening instead of just dumping a mountain of truth on someone.

Bill responded to our suggestions and his people noticed an immediate change in his communication style and demeanor. We asked Bill why he was not able to see his ability to teach and communicate. Bill felt his inability to communicate stemmed in large part because he came from a family who had a rule that "Children should be seen and not heard." That rule became a belief that held him back in life and in his work.

Bill now writes training procedures and programs, trains staff in import regulations, and is often sought after to bring his knowledge and expertise to trade shows. Gone is the "do it my way" bully, and hello to teacher Bill. Bravo, Bill!

We have so many success stories about how the Core Power System™ has successfully changed people and companies. As a side note, we often start our assessment process with the CEO because they so often exhibit the tone and tenor of the company. We have coached many CEOs so they have a more powerful picture of themselves.

Here is a brief description of the eight competencies for the Core Power System™.

Compassionist

Always looking for a way to aid others. They love a cause to get behind. Compassionate acts of kindness light them up!

Builder

Builders want to make/build things. They love to grow things. You find your skydivers and zip liners in this group.

Organizer

Organizers love balance and beauty. They love organized systems and tend toward perfectionism.

Diplomat

They are your *people* people. People are drawn to them and seek to be near them. Strangers will tell them their life story.

Communicator

They are natural teachers and explainers of all things. Words and communicating come easy to them.

Truth Teller

Truth is important to them as is keeping the record straight. They are often blunt and straight to the point kind of people.

Mover and Shaker

Let's get it done is their motto. They need freedom and choices. They are often leading and rarely following.

Philosopher

These are your bigger picture people packed with plenty of common sense. They want people to take their advice because they just know how things will turn out.

Culture Officer

The *Culture Officer* is an important person in a company, especially if a company is committed to keeping its Culture healthy. If that describes your company, then you can't do that without a Culture Officer as part of your team. You'll note we use the term "Culture Officer." We do so intentionally because this individual must be a member of the senior leadership team in order to be effective. He/she must have direct access to the CEO or the COO, otherwise their perceived power and influence is diminished.

You have to see the value in what they can bring to your company. Think of them like any other professional, be it an engineer, financial strategist or CEO. A Culture Officer needs to be able to see into the future when it comes to trends. They have to be able to think and explore options, make good choices and recommendations, and truly have at their heart what is good for the company, its customers, suppliers and employees.

A Culture Officer can draw from their life experiences, the experiences of others, and can seek information from many internal and external sources to aid them in keeping your organization headed in the right direction. They need to be the keepers of the truth and capable of standing in the line of fire when it comes to telling senior leaders the facts and protecting the values and principles of the organization.

When it comes to managing reputational risk, the Culture Officer needs to be tireless in their efforts to run interference and pivot when major decisions are being made and Culture shifts are anticipated. In many companies the Culture Officer works independently while reporting directly to the CEO or COO. We believe the Culture Officer should be a confidant and close ally of all senior executives.

We encourage our clients to make the Culture Officer a member of the senior management team. Each member of the management team is an expert in their areas and, as such, becomes a valued resource to the Culture Officer. Only when they all work together can a company manage to avoid the risks that often plague an organization.

At CRI Global CAPS, we are frequently asked to help companies outline the duties of a Culture Officer in accordance with the construction of the company's *Culture Playbook*, making recruiting for the position much easier. One of the steps we recommend is for every Culture Officer to join their professional organization. We are active in the nonprofit association, the International Chief Culture Officers Association which can be accessed at: www.IACCO.org

We believe seeking out and putting into place conscious business tools will help your company raise its level of consciousness to positively impact your bottom line.

Conscious Business Take-Aways:

1. Conscious businesses raise the level of success in their companies by using conscious business tools.

2. Conscious business tools include: Assessments, *Culture Playbooks*, the Core Power System™ and hiring a Culture Officer.

3. Avoiding reputational risk comes from successfully managing your Culture.

Chapter 13

The Culture Playbook:
Why You Need It and How to Use the Five Ps
to Transform Your Business

Two years ago we received a phone call on a rare rainy southern California afternoon. On the phone were the Chief Operations Officer and Chief Financial Officer of a large financial institution. They wanted to ask us some questions about Culture and, specifically, how managing Culture could best be done to protect their reputational risk.

Their interest in managing Culture was triggered by their internal auditors. The executives explained that the internal auditors were charged with two important functions. First, they were to look for risks in their financial practices across all areas of the company. Second, they were charged with alerting management of any emerging trends in the financial services oversight processes that could have an adverse impact on the company's performance. The executives explained that during their most recent internal audit, a potential risk or threat was identified. That threat could negatively impact the financial institution's reputation so senior management needed to find ways to prevent the company from becoming the victim of reputational risk should certain conditions or negative publicity reach its customers.

The executives explained to us that as financial institutions grow, it becomes imperative to protect their reputation so as to

191

avoid losing customers which, in turn, would negatively impact their performance and bottom line. The executives needed to construct a plan for managing and measuring reputational risk. The auditors indicated it would be to their advantage if management could proactively show to state and federal regulators that they had a proven way to measure reputational risk should the financial institution be audited on this subject.

They asked us if it could be done through a Culture Assessment™. We assured the executives it could be done and, furthermore, a Culture Assessment would not only be useful in measuring and preventing reputational risk but it would also be the first step toward constructing a *Culture Playbook* to manage the process.

We explained that a *Culture Playbook* is a written document that uses the Five Ps of Culture – Purpose, Principles, People, Processes and Performance – as a roadmap for managing risk. The level of detail and the depth of review for each of the Five Ps depended on their business and its respective tolerance for risk. We have worked with companies that have created *Culture Playbook*s of 20 pages and some with 200 pages. While every *Culture Playbook* includes the Five Ps, the process varies widely for each company because no two businesses are the same. Every business has its own unique Culture and the Five Ps are unique to that particular company or organization. Thus, no two *Culture Playbook*s will be the same. The only thing that is consistent is the use of the Five Ps because they form the foundation and framework of your organization.

Over the past twenty years, we have learned that regardless of whether a company is large or small, every company can benefit from creating a *Culture Playbook*. As consultants, we witness the relief our clients experience from constructing a *Culture Playbook* that provides form and structure to a concept that has been untamed and unmanaged simply because senior management didn't understand how to leverage their company's Culture as a competitive force, and use it to win more customers and increase profits. After years of dealing with Culture and refining the *Culture Playbook*, we now possess that know-how.

Whether it takes two weeks or two months to put the elements into place, the bottom line will be better served by adding this focus to your conscious business methodologies. Once it's constructed, your *Culture Playbook* will serve you for a long time. Of course, you need to make sure you follow it and revisit it regularly, and you'll need to update your *Culture Playbook* whenever you change your business model or introduce major new products that alter how your company performs.

Also, when projects are initiated or products change, as new divisions are added, when your business changes in response to a shifting global marketplace, when competition heats up, when employees are added or when a new generation of customers emerges, your *Culture Playbook* needs to be reviewed and updated. It's important to understand your *Culture Playbook* is not a static concept or tool. Just as your business is a living, breathing corpus, so too is your *Culture Playbook*.

We have also learned that building a *Culture Playbook* affords a company the opportunity to see how their business is put together and if they have strayed from their core business principles and values. If so, your *Culture Playbook* is designed to help you get back on track. As we follow the data abuse scandal that has rocked Facebook, we wonder a few things. First, we wonder if Facebook had a *Culture Playbook*. Second, if Facebook had a *Culture Playbook*, was it current? Third, did their *Culture Playbook* include a review of Facebook's privacy practices and did it identify potential threats? If

Facebook had a *Culture Playbook*, we believe they could have avoided the recent hit to their reputation by not protecting their users' data information.

Putting together a *Culture Playbook* is not a difficult process because the Five Ps provide the framework and guideline to build it. When your *Culture Playbook* is finished, it offers the company a tangible way to manage risk of all kinds, especially reputational risk. What is most unique about a *Culture Playbook* is that it serves as a conscious business tool because it requires your company to consider more than just the bottom line. It requires your company to consider the heart and soul of your organization – your people and the various jobs they perform. This includes employees, customers and suppliers.

How to Manage Your Culture Playbook

While we've helped many clients create their *Culture Playbook*s and use it as a tool to increase employee engagement, customer retention and performance, we've also witnessed a number of companies who have hired us to go through the process because "Culture" was the "Flavor-on-the-Month" topic. So let's be frank. If that's your attitude, don't waste your money on developing a *Culture Playbook*. Just keep your fingers crossed that your company doesn't get ambushed by imposter clients like Facebook did with Cambridge Analytica, or one of your employees doesn't turn out to be another Edward Snowden, the American computer professional who copied and leaked classified information to the Chinese and Russians and now lives in Russia.

We've also witnessed a number of our clients who failed to properly maintain this valuable tool. We found two reasons that most often contributed to the abandonment. First, they failed to make a commitment to keeping their *Culture Playbook* updated. It never works when a proven business method goes into the dark zone. In other words, out of sight, out of mind. That's what we mean by PDZ – Project Dead Zone. Regrettably, this practice happens too frequently in business because leadership is either not committed to its Culture or another Flavor-of-the-Month comes along and distracts management. If you don't believe in the danger of allowing your Culture to end up in the PDZ, just watch the evening news or read a major newspaper. Every week there's a story about some company, university, government agency or non-profit organization that has run afoul because they ignored one of the Five Ps and allowed their Culture to atrophy at the expense of their reputation.

In all our previous detailed examples, the afflicted business suffered serious negative exposure to its bottom line due to reputational risk. It's the classic example that one hand doesn't know – or care – what the other hand is doing. The primary reason for many of the corporate debacles we've cited in this book boils down to one important missing element. The company failed to appoint a team or individual to protect their Culture and manage their *Culture Playbook* – that's assuming they even had one in the first place, which we doubt.

This brings us to the second reason why companies get into trouble and suffer a loss of reputation; senior management fails to buy into the process of continued Culture reviews across the entire organization. For a *Culture Playbook* to protect your company from risk, there needs to be a process that will connect your company's Culture with its employees, customers and suppliers so everyone is involved and committed to protecting your company's reputation and Culture at all costs.

Remember, it only takes one or two misguided employees to mess up the whole works and derail your company. Wells Fargo knows this to be true as does Starbucks, a company that spent a small fortune retraining its entire workforce because two African American men were unduly arrested and escorted out of a downtown Philadelphia Starbucks for loitering and trespassing when they didn't order any food or drinks.

Regardless of whether Starbucks was within its legal rights to have the two men removed from the store, the social media backlash against the socially progressive Seattle-based company damaged its once-sterling reputation.

From a Culture perspective, our question is very simple. Why did this happen in the first place? Did an overzealous employee simply act outside the boundaries or did Starbucks fail as a company to adopt rules and procedures for non-paying customers? Haven't we all used a Starbuck's restroom for convenience without placing an order?

Again, these are the kinds of embarrassing issues and unexpected situations that should have been addressed by management and would have been part of a company's *Culture Playbook*. Certainly Starbucks does not condone discrimination or the mistreatment of its customers and guests. But when one or two employees "go rogue" and create this kind of havoc, all hell can break loose. This is what your *Culture Playbook* is designed to address and prevent.

At CRI Global CAPS, we have seen many companies create their own variation of a *Culture Playbook* then implement an oversight process but fail to get a company-wide commitment to that process. For whatever reason, at the highest levels of the company, the continued oversight process was not a priority. Perhaps, in an effort to save money, the process for updating their *Culture Playbook* was often delegated to a department or team that didn't have the time, interest, understanding, commitment or resources for managing the company's Culture process.

Too often we have seen companies make the mistake of entrusting their *Culture Playbook* to the human resources department. As we noted earlier, while human resources plays an important role in an organization, it is not the right place to house your *Culture Playbook*. The function of human resources has shifted dramatically in recent years. It seems the human resources department's primary function is to manage the Three Rs – Recruit, Retain and Release. HR manages your risk as it relates to your people. HR should not be a default place where management places the trust and care of the company's *Culture Playbook*.

So what do you do to manage your *Culture Playbook*? Again, we recommend to our clients that they hire a Culture Officer and place this individual in senior operations or an internal audit area. Give them the power and tools to work across all areas of your company. At CRI Global CAPS, we have found the best solution is to keep your Culture Officer autonomous from other departments and have him/her report directly to senior management through the COO or the CEO.

Companies that are serious about managing their reputational risk need to take the process seriously and create the necessary system to manage the process. The mindset of the company's leadership will greatly impact this process. If you are serious about becoming a conscious business, you need to change your mindset as it relates to the construction and management of your *Culture Playbook*.

It Just Takes a Small Step in a Different Direction

CRI Global CAPS has helped many companies grow, improve their performance, and prosper through innovation and training. Our clients inherently know when it's time to makes changes so their company performs better. We value our clients who make a commitment to change and follow through on their commitment to Culture. It takes both courage and stamina to do so.

Several years ago a client asked for our help to improve communication among employees who were struggling in one of their divisions. We determined a training session using our Core Power personality profile would help them. We brought the division together and conducted a series of training sessions then reviewed their results and got their managers working with the tools we provided them. We brainstormed ways to get each person to recognize other people's core powers, talents and communication styles. We created visible reminders, including buttons and door plaques that identified their dominant core powers. We gave them team dynamic exercises to keep the process going until it became second nature for everyone to understand each person's core powers.

We returned three months later to measure and evaluate the progress and determine how well the information was being used, and what impact was made to enhance performance and communication. Much to our disappointment, there had been no follow-through. The reason was traced to the Division Director, Sally, who did not buy into the process despite her assurances at the outset. We learned Sally felt threatened by the training process that was dictated by senior management because her division was under-performing. We also learned that because Sally felt threatened, she didn't hold her managers accountable for any changes or improvements that we designed.

Frankly, we were upset because no one at a senior level thought to get Sally's buy-in before launching the training program, including us! When we discussed the lack of results with her, Sally bluntly told us we had wasted our time, her time and her company's money. We agreed, but we didn't give up, nor did we give in to her excuses. We challenged Sally to let us help her raise the performance bar under her terms and conditions so she owned the program and was in charge of its success. Sally eventually agreed, as did her COO.

Although we only made modest changes in the training and project design, the biggest change was the most important – the buy-in and support of the division director. Now we worked FOR Sally and WITH Sally! We didn't need to spend much time convincing her that communication was essential to any company's success nor did we have to explain that her division's bottom line could be negatively impacted by a lack of proper communication. She already knew that! Sally was a smart and shrewd person who understood all the benefits of what we were trying to accomplish. The hurdle for us was simply to create an air of trust and get Sally's buy-in. We needed to create a trust bond with her and assure Sally that we were on her side. We created the trust bond by introducing Sally to her Core Power profile and how she could best leverage her powers to raise her performance and the performance of her team. Once we built that trust bond with her, there was no stopping her!

With the blessing of the COO, we put Sally through a crash course and brought her up to speed. When we returned six weeks later, we found a complete transformation in her division's performance, attitude and communication levels. People were talking solutions to problems and making fewer mistakes. Shipments were being processed right the first time. And, most important to the division manager and her bosses, the division's numbers were trending toward the black for the first time in 14 months. Everyone was happy! Other results were also visible. Employee morale and engagement were higher, and fewer people were transferring or quitting. It should come as no surprise that when people get along at work, performance and morale improves.

Buy-in to process improvement is essential to the success of any initiative. One key person who is out of step with any process improvement initiative can derail the entire mission. If you're going to construct a *Culture Playbook,* as a company, everyone needs to buy into a yearly Culture Assessment and periodic adjustments. Commitment and buy-in to any process improvement are two of the most important elements in becoming and staying a conscious business.

Six Steps to Constructing a Culture Playbook

The construction of a *Culture Playbook* is a delicate process because it requires a commitment of time, resources and money, as well as a dedicated focus on all the key areas of your company. You cannot afford to ignore any aspect of your business that could negatively impact your reputation or jeopardize your customer loyalty. Just consider the Starbuck's episode in Philadelphia or the damage to United Airlines' reputation as a result of the Dr. Dao fiasco. This is why every employee must understand the importance of reputational risk and buy into the concept of a *Culture Playbook.* It only takes one iceberg to sink your ship!

As we mentioned, when constructing your *Culture Playbook,* the same five steps are used with every business. The depth of detail and complexity within your business determines the length of the *Culture Playbook.* Here's a brief sample of the steps we use to create a customized *Culture Playbook*:

1. Conduct a Culture Assessment across the company or within a specific division(s).

2. Review the details of the assessment with senior management to determine where on the Culture Spectrum your company falls. Determine where in the Five Ps of Culture you face the greatest risk of exposure.

3. Appoint a Culture champion – someone who is senior in your organization and a true believer with a "can do" attitude. Together we determine the overall scope and depth of review necessary to avoid reputational risk and ensure high performance. Next, we ask senior management to appoint a support team to begin the process of defining the parameters as we review each of the Five Ps.

4. Draft the *Culture Playbook* parameters. Present it to your senior team for their review and approval.

5. Review the finished *Culture Playbook* and make any final additions/changes to it. Decide on how often management will meet to discuss the ongoing review of your *Culture Playbook*.

6. Host an all-hands meeting or a series of meetings led by the CEO or another senior company officer to discuss the importance of the *Culture Playbook* and the roles and responsibilities each and every employee has in protecting the company's reputation and Culture.

These are the basic steps. They may change depending on a client's specific needs, but in the end, you will have a robust *Culture Playbook*. Our goal is simple. We want you to provide your people with a viable document that serves as a framework for aligning your performance with your conscious business goals and, in the process, avoid reputational risk while strengthening your bottom line and boosting customer loyalty.

Conscious Business Take-Aways:

1. Constructing a *Culture Playbook* will help you to define and manage reputational risk.
2. *Culture Playbooks* are only effective when managed properly. You need a senior manager to lead the process then create a companywide commitment to the continued focus on the process.
3. Using the Five Ps of Culture to construct your *Culture Playbook* is a conscious business practice that will positively impact your bottom line.

Chapter 14
Closing Thoughts on Culture

While the success of every business and organization hinges on several key factors, we believe the foundation of success begins with a strong Culture built on the Five Ps. We have also learned from our time in the field with clients several valuable lessons that we'd like to offer you in the hopes that these lessons help you achieve your goals more easily and quickly. We think these lessons apply to every organization. Here they are:

A Leader's List of Conscious Business Principles

1. Make a commitment to become a conscious business. It will require you to change your perception and recognize people before profits. It will also require you to initiate change within your company. This will not be simple because most people resist change, especially when they cannot foretell what will happen.

2. Value your people. If you take care of your people, they will help you take care of the bottom line as well as the top line. Always put your people before profits.

3. Encourage people to carry the message to the top, regardless of whether they bear good news or bad news. Information is powerful. The better informed you are, the sooner you can respond to problems and solve them. Don't shoot the

messenger! It kills morale and creates unnecessary reputational risks.

4. Frequently ask your employees, customers and suppliers for their opinions and suggestions then implement the ones that make sense.

5. Listen to smart people, but always remember they are human and, therefore, fallible. Think for yourself.

6. No leader has all the answers to all the questions and most leaders don't always know the right questions to ask or how to ask the right questions. So build a strong team of honest people who are willing to tell you the truth. Then listen to what they're telling you.

7. Never discount the message because you discount the messenger.

8. Facts are friendly, sometimes harsh, but always fair.

9. Gathering data is important because it allows you to create information. Information leads to knowledge, and knowledge helps you make the right decisions. We call this process "Wisdom."

10. Leaders build strong teams comprised of diverse thinkers and personalities, not a bunch of "yes men." A leader's success is enhanced by a strong, diverse team.

11. Givers gain. Give of yourself before you ask others to make a major commitment or sacrifice. Remember, leaders lead. They don't ask permission, they just do it!

12. Encourage your people to network and be connected in their community and professional organizations. This is what successful leaders expect of their people and this is how successful organizations behave and perform. They are involved, engaged and visible.

13. Always be working on the next thing. Don't let today's problems and challenges slow you down to the point that you lose your forward momentum or stop thinking about the next important goal or task.

14. Eat crow. Sometimes we say or do stupid things. Sometimes we make bad decisions. When this happens, be the kind of leader who steps forward and says, "I blew it!" "It was my bad." "I'm sorry." Practice humility and have the courage to be wrong as much as you are right.

15. Think less, do more! Think more, react less.

16. Allow yourself to dream and daydream. Imagine. Wander. Take a nap.

17. Allow yourself to be the butt of a joke. Lighten up. Get dunked in the water tank at the company picnic once a year! It's good for your image.

18. Encourage people to challenge your thinking and conclusions. It strengthens your resolve and sometimes it opens your mind to new possibilities.

19. Lead by example. No organization survives for long by creating a Culture of fear and intimidation. It merely breeds confusion, discord and a sense of loyalty to self – none of which is positive.

20. Share the credit when you succeed, but not the blame when you fail.

21. As the leader, if you continue to plug away in the face of adversity, others will follow your lead. If you give up, so will your team. Never quit.

22. Culture trumps strategy.

About the Authors

Tom Hinton is the President and CEO of CRI Global CAPS, LLC based in San Diego, California. Tom is recognized as one of America's most sought-after conscious business speakers and consultants in the areas of Creating a Culture of Excellence in the Workplace, Life Balance, Customer Service and Employee Engagement. As president of CRI Global CAPS, Tom leads a dynamic and seasoned team that helps clients assess their Culture and make refinements to improve their people, performance and profitability.

Tom's high-energy and content-rich presentations make him a popular speaker at corporate, association and personal development conferences. Since 1989, he has addressed over 1,300 corporate, association, and government audiences in the United States, Canada, Germany, Austria, Japan, Mexico, Ireland, Spain, Portugal, France, England, Scotland, China, Singapore, Turkey, Lithuania, Croatia, South Africa, Australia and New Zealand.

Tom is the author of *The Spirit of Service, Leadership Lessons I Learned on the Links: 72 Ways to Par the Course of Business and Life; 10,000 Days: The Rest of Your Life, the Best of Your Life;* and *Passages: A Book of Daily Inspiration.* He is also the co-author, along with Wini Schaeffer, of *Customer Focused Quality: What to Do on Monday Morning.*

Barbara Yager, J.D. As the Operational Director of Consulting at CRI Global CAPS, LLC, Barbara is rated as one of America's foremost thought leaders on helping companies create a conscious and engaged workplace environment.

Barbara has developed a series of high-level practices and training programs designed to guide senior executives and entrepreneurs to the power of Culture and use that power to strengthen corporate performance and results. Barbara is the creator of the *Culture Spectrum*™ as well as the developer of The *Culture Playbook*™ and the Core Power Assessment™ tools that are used by numerous companies today.

Having spent nearly 25 years in the world of corporate law and finance, Barbara understands the key role senior leaders play in developing a *High-Performance Culture*, making tough decisions and effectively managing risk.

Barbara's philosophy can be summed-up as follows: when employees perform at their best, they naturally have the best interests of the company at heart. Her message has a simple theme: Culture is about creating positive energy in the workplace and using that positive energy to achieve outstanding results. When this happens, your people will perform at higher levels and profits will increase.

Barbara is also a sought-after professional speaker on the topics of Creating a Conscious Business, Relationship Building, How to Create a High Energy Workplace and Culture Shift: Why Corporate Cultures Change and How to Manage that Shift. She divides her time between San Diego, CA and Madison, CT.

CRI Global CAPS, LLC

CRI Global CAPS, LLC is a dynamic international training and consulting firm established in 1987 and headquartered in San Diego, CA. We specialize in helping clients identify, strengthen and leverage their culture to achieve three key outcomes:

- ❖ Minimize Reputational Risk by creating a Culture Blueprint and other strategies to guide your senior-level decision-making.
- ❖ Engage your employees to increase their workplace productivity, commitment and internal harmony.
- ❖ Strengthen customer and supplier loyalty to boost your bottom line.

At CRI Global CAPS, we focus on corporate culture assessments, developing culture systems and strategies, and helping clients successfully implement those culture systems and strategies. Thus, our acronym "CAPS" – Culture Assessments & Performance Systems.

We believe a company's performance and profitability are tied closely to a company's culture.

In today's competitive workplace, a company's standards, values and attitudes directly impact the bottom line. We created the Culture Spectrum™, a valuable tool to gauge where your company stands in terms of its culture. We also created the Culture Playbook so companies can design their own customized Culture Blueprint™.

What We Do

CRI Global CAPS will help your company make the transition to a conscious business, assess its culture, design a customized Culture Playbook™, and implement that Culture Playbook™ to improve performance and increase profitability. We provide a range of culture assessment services to Boards and Senior Executives using our Culture Spectrum™ system.

Our Goal

Our goal is to provide you with an unvarnished analysis of your cultural strengths, areas for improvement, and a winning plan to integrate your Culture Playbook™ with your Business Strategies and Profitability Segments.

Contact Us

For more information on our service, please contact us at: Info@CRIGlobalCAPS.com or call us at (1) 858-449-9055. Our website is: www.CRIGlobalCAPS.com.

www.ingramcontent.com/pod-product-compliance
Lightning Source LLC
Chambersburg PA
CBHW060551200326
41521CB00007B/548